# THE ULTIMATE ANTI-BULLYING SOLUTIONS GUIDE

## THE SURE FIRE WAY TO STOP BULLYING NOW!

ANITA TELLE

ISBN:9781928155362

PUBLISHED BY:
10-10-10 PUBLISHING
MARKHAM, ON
CANADA

# Contents

# Acknowledgements

Mom and Dad, thank you for teaching me to reach for the stars; Teaching me to trust in God and know that everyone is unique and special, and that life's adventure is a gift to all mankind, no matter where you are or who you are.

Mr. Ward, you are an amazing teacher with a big heart. Thank you for allowing me to interview you and share some of your expertise in anti-bullying solutions.

John Harten, thank you for your patience in editing my book. Your insight as a teacher was greatly appreciated.

Dr. Garner, you have a huge heart, and the world is a better place because you are in it. Thank you for all you do for children with deformities, giving them the possibility to have a normal life. Your positive outlook on life and "can do" attitude is clearly one of the reasons so many children you have helped  can have a normal life.

My family and friends, thank you for always encouraging me and being there for me.

To all the elementary school teachers who opened up and shared stories, as well as inviting me to share my message and books in your classroom.

My dear friends at Santa Cruz Children's Charities. We are making a difference in the world!

And to my little ray of sunshine, Branden – I love you with all my heart.

# Letter from Dr. Steven L. Garner

As a plastic surgeon, I have devoted my life to reconstructing both normal appearance and normal function to people and to body parts afflicted by injury or disease. The specialty of plastic surgery has offered me emotional rewards and personal satisfaction I could not achieve doing destructive surgical procedures such as tumor removal or amputations. It was a good choice, as most of my days at work are truly amazing.

Some days are not so good, days that make me want to run and hide, find another less stressful livelihood, or even just cry. Mother Nature is a most independent lady who we may be able to influence but never truly control. Not every disease can be cured, and not every treatment course goes well even if everything is done perfectly.

On one of my worst career days, I was moping around our community shopping mall at lunchtime feeling low down. The burn out I was experiencing was reaching peak levels, and I was near the end of my rope. Off in the distance, I saw a mall kiosk that put personal photos on coffee mugs or on aprons as a gift for family. Something about one of the display aprons caught my eye as being very attractive. As I moved closer, I saw that it was a head shot photo of an adorable blonde little boy saying, "I love you, Grandma!" in Norwegian. Suddenly, I realized that the child was the author's adopted son and my patient Branden, brought to the USA from Ukraine as a toddler with a completely unrepaired and severe bilateral cleft lip and palate (which is far more than twice the severity of a unilateral cleft). I had repaired his lip and palate several years earlier but had not seen him for a while. Now he was so cute that merchants wanted to use his appearance to sell their wares. Words can never adequately express the depth of emotion and professional renewal I felt at that moment, a moment that in and by itself made every step I took and sacrifice I made to become a plastic surgeon well worth it. I went right back to work feeling renewed.

What in the world does that have to do with a book on bullying? Forty years ago, I personally was right in the middle of a junior high group of students that regularly teased and tormented a little girl with a repaired bilateral cleft lip and palate. I didn't understand why her speech sounded strange or why her lip and nose looked unusual. Twenty years later as a plastic surgeon, I saw her photograph in a surgery textbook written by my mentor and teacher S. Anthony Wolfe, MD. The shame I felt at that moment and even still today just won't ever leave me. Let this be my long overdue and very sincere apology to Judy in Miami. We are all (even doctors!) capable of bullying, sexist, racist, and cruel behavior, but we also are all equally capable of extreme kindness and citizenship. I applaud Anita for writing this book and invite all who read it to join me in being part of the solutions in this world and not part of the problems. We have a choice.

Steven L. Garner, M.D., F.A.C.S
Santa Cruz, CA

## Chapter 1
## Once upon a time in the land of (perceived) perfect

In the land of perfect, all is well, there is no ugly, no pain: just the joy and gratitude of a beautiful life. And it's all good.

I like that, I buy into that and I want that. Don't we all? Then again, what is a perfect life for you might not be a perfect life for me; you like to climb mountains, I like to sail on the open seas. You like to ride a horse; I like to ride a bike. That's the magic of who we are, the beauty of being different; with different interests we are able to access many different opportunities, ways to take our special gifts and make them stand out. This we all understand. On this level we can see clearly that different is good; we certainly would not want everyone to do the same thing we like to do. It would be a boring world if everyone walked around in the same shoes, same jacket and same pants. Individuality is a plus, and we should appreciate difference and celebrate our diversity.

The reality is that when we decide that everything is black or white, there is no grey. We create breeding grounds for FEAR and mistrust, and when we do that, we state that diversity and difference are something to fear, and human nature says: what we fear, we must destroy.

This seems so obvious; however, it is unfortunate that when it comes down to the issue on a deep level, most of us DO fear "different." We feel safer and more in charge when we do not have to deal with something or someone who does not share our beliefs or our value system, our interests or nationality. We feel uneasy with those things. There is, however, ONE thing that is the same for everyone wherever you live or whatever social ranking you are, and that is the right for every human being to feel safe, have enough to eat, have friends, family, the right to freedom, education, religion, etc. I believe that a lot of prejudice comes from a lack of daring to step outside our own comfort zone and experience.

From very early on in our lives, movies, books and fairytales tell us about Prince Charming and the knight in shining armor, and the beautiful princess who does not want to kiss a frog, and about having it all. From the school we go to, to college, girlfriends/ boyfriends, marriage/ partner, children, grandchildren, vacation homes, world travels, to the perfect home with a white picket fence. We cannot always arrive at this perfect place in the timeframe we set for ourselves. Therefore, there is an enormous amount of pressure which we choose to put on ourselves to fit in. This amount of pressure that we willingly put on ourselves is in an effort to not fall behind; we will do whatever is necessary to fit into the cookie-cutter image of what society says is normal, and what we feel is expected of us. The toll this can take on our health, relationships and our children is often ignored, because to admit it can in many ways make us believe we are not up to par with where we should be at this precise time in our life.

As we continue the journey, we see that the land of perfect might be a little overrated, and the sacrifices we make to live in the land of perfect can stress us and make us feel we only exist rather than living. It truly is important that we do realize and keep all this in mind as we look at our busy lives and evaluate where we are. Did we ever think that in the land of perfect we were one day going to have to deal with bullies? That we would have to deal with tears, frustration and helplessness as we see our children being hurt and bullied, their tear-stained faces as they tell us about their day, how they do not want to go back to school, and "Why does it always happen to me?" Well, that is, if you are lucky enough to have a child that communicates instead of hiding it all inside. What we are looking for is to have some peace of mind in the safe sanctuary called our home, our little cocoon which now has been invaded by ugly stories of bullies, the little box sitting on the table in our safe home, the box named computer, which allows our children to be bullied on line even in their safe home, the frustration of not knowing what to do.

The struggle of wondering if we are over reacting, and the belief we should be able to deal with this in a fast and controlled manner, saying things like, "There is no reason for anyone to know about this. It's nothing to worry about. It will all go away. It's just part of growing up."

I feel it is accurate to say that none of us are prepared to deal with bullies. The reality is that we think it's going to happen to everyone else but us, however, when it does happen to us, we often times don't know what to do, and oftentimes we decided to poo poo the whole thing, brush it under the rug, tell our child to be strong, just plain deal with it. Most of us are not doing this to be mean or insensitive; we are doing this because we do not know what to do and the tools we have to work with are not sufficient.

Unfortunately, many of us feel that the schools, teachers and therapists should be the ones to deal with the issue of bullying, because they have the education, and "probably deal with this kind of stuff all the time." Surely it happens at school most of the time? Therefore, we might think, that's the place that needs to deal with it. However, if we take some time and really evaluate the situation, we know in our heart that it is *our* responsibility, so now it comes down to What can I do? What are my options? In this book, I have given you some tools to use, including free downloads, prewritten letters so the only thing you have to do is "fill in the blanks." I have even included a letter of apology, should your daughter or son be the bully.

Well, what exactly is the definition of bullying, you might ask? To ensure that you have the definition completely clear, here is what stopbullying.gov gives us as the definition:

*Bullying is unwanted, aggressive behavior among school-aged children that involves a real or perceived power imbalance. The behavior is repeated, or has the potential to be repeated, over time. Both kids who are bullied and who bully others may have serious, lasting problems. In order to be considered bullying, the behavior must be aggressive and include:*

*An imbalance of power: Kids who bully use their power such as physical strength, access to embarrassing information or popularity to control or harm others. Power imbalances can change over time and in different situations, even if they involve the same people.*

*Repetition: Bullying behaviors happen more than once or have the potential to happen more than once. Bullying includes actions such as making threats, spreading rumors, attacking someone physically or verbally, and excluding someone from a group on purpose.*

When considering a subject such as bullying, one cannot get away from statistics, so I wanted to share some. Every year, 2.7

million students report that they are being bullied. These numbers continue to rise. Schools are trying to deal with it, coaches are doing their best to prevent it, therapists work with the problem, but the numbers still continue to grow, and with the introduction of cyber bullying, bullying is no longer limited to the playground.

What exactly is cyber bullying, or online bullying you might ask? We are dealing with two types of cyber bullying: real time (synchronic) such as chat rooms, instant messaging, online games, cell phones; and delayed cyber bullying (asynchronous). Asynchronous cyber bullying includes emails, Facebook, blogs, Instagram, and other social networks. You must make sure your children guard all their passwords and change their password if they think it has been jeopardized. Teach them never to give out their password to "friends" who then give it out to their friends, and pretty soon it is a mess. It is also very easy to block a person from your social media device, and children should be encouraged to do just that if they are bullied. Make sure you reinforce for them the importance of telling an adult if they are bullied.

An online bully can wreck someone's reputation by stealing someone's online identity; they will then use that identity to send out hurtful messages, etc. They can create fake Facebook pages, or blogs with the sole purpose of embarrassing and hurting someone else. At times, an online bully might just be someone who tries to embarrass, push around and intimidate children who are online playing an online video game. Amongst gamers, such a bully is called a "griefer."

Kids can post nasty pictures or messages about others on blogs, websites and social media; they can even pretend to be someone else so that you don't even know who it is that's saying these horrible things about you. They can spread rumors on social networks and harass you by text messaging and emails. As of right now, most cyber bullying takes place amongst teenagers, however, the younger children are when they receive access to cell phones, email, and iPads, the sooner they will be introduced to this kind of ugliness, and the easier it is for children at a much younger age to be cyber bullied. They have no knowledge or tools to help them understand what is going on, and most of the time they do not even understand that they are being bullied; they just know that someone on the Internet, text or email does not like them, they are mean, and it really hurts to know that they're not liked.

However, they may worry, "If I tell my mom and dad they might get mad and take my phone away, and then my 'lifeline' to my world has disappeared, and I might even get bullied because I do not have my phone any more."

More than one in three young people have experienced cyber threats online. Over 25% of adolescents and teens have been bullied repeatedly through their cell phones. 50% of young people do not tell their parents when cyber bullying occurs. They are afraid they might lose their cell phones, and they are more afraid of losing their phones than of the internal damage bullying does. We know that being the victim of bullying can lead to other problems such as trouble in school, depression, drug abuse, etc. Over 80% of all teenagers use their cell phones on a regular basis. It is the most popular device amongst teenagers and a very easy place for cyber bullying to take place.

Continuing on with statistics, looking at offline bullying, an eye opener for me was the fact that about 160,000 children miss school every day out of the fear of being bullied. 56% of all students say they have witnessed bullying taking place at school. The top school years for being bullied are fourth through eighth grade; however, this is different when it comes to cyber bullying.

Within the gay community, it is reported that 80% of the youth have been harassed or threatened, and 25% have been physically attacked.

According to stopbullying.gov, a large study found the following percentage of middle schools students had experienced bullying in these locations at school: classroom (29.3%); hallway or lockers (29%); cafeteria (23.4%); gym or PE class (19.5%); bathroom (12.2%); playground or recess (6.2%).

The students also reported that they had experienced these various types of bullying: name calling (44.2%); teasing (43.3%); spreading rumors or lies (36.3%); pushing or shoving (32.4%); hitting, slapping, or kicking (29.2%); leaving out (28.5%); threatening (27.4%); stealing belongings (27.3%); sexual comments or gestures (23.7%); email or blogging (9.9%).

The study also reported that most bullying takes place in school, outside on school grounds, and on the school bus. Bullying also happens wherever kids gather in the community. And, of course, cyber bullying occurs on cell phones and online.

Bullying and teenage suicide have been in the news a lot lately. More children die from suicide in the 15-19 age group than from the top six medical causes of death combined. Suicide is the 3rd leading cause of death for both the 10-14 and the 15-19 age groups in the United States. 28% of students nationwide reported feeling so sad or hopeless almost every day for two or more weeks in a row that they stopped doing some of their usual activities. It is important to know that half of all lifelong mental illnesses begin before age 14. The very scary thing is that 80% of all youth with mental illness are not identified and do not receive any mental health services. Even though bullying has been partially to blame for suicides, it tends to be more the "straw that broke the camel's back" than the only reason for it. A child does not take their own life for only one reason. We must be very careful with the sensationalizing of this issue that the media feeds us. They are out to report something shocking, and oftentimes do not do any form of involved research before coming to a conclusion that bullying was or is the only problem. Statistics show that 90% of people who die by suicide have depression and other mental disorders; however it is a preventable and treatable problem. (Ref: National Institute of Mental Health)

The subject on child/teen suicide is way beyond my expertise and should be left to the professionals to deal with. However, I have included some website addresses for further research and a list of warning signs, etc. on my website and also in the back of the book. Responding effectively to bullying comes down to the need to educate ourselves.

When you read these statistics and see the numbers in black and white, you realize how serious these problems are. I feel very comfortable in saying that there is light in the end of the tunnel. I know we as parents can make a big change, and there are a lot of wonderful websites and organizations that can help. I believe that the more educated we are on the subject, the better equipped we are to help our children. We must be realistic about what is going on in our schools, on the Internet, in emails, on cell phones and on the playground. Statistics show that only 20-30% of students who are bullied tell an adult about it. We must ask more questions, understand policies, understand what our children's rights are, get involved and communicate with our children. The more we do, the more empowered we will feel. Ask open-ended questions, questions that do not allow a simple yes or no answer, maybe something like: "What did you like the most about school today?" "What was the most frustrating thing that happened at school today?" Make sure you know your child's friends. Personally, I have made it a habit to talk to my son about his day on the way home from school. I also repeat back to my son what I hear him say. This helps him correct something I might have misunderstood, or add to something he was telling me. I also ask him who he played with that day, etc. Let's get back to where we started in this chapter, in the land of perfect. It is the land where dreams come true, and a place where we all would like to live. I believe with all my heart that we can get there. We can have the life we want, we can make a difference and the more people who get involved, the sooner we can get there. We all wish that we did live in the land of perfect, and by taking the first steps, we are on our way there, and also on our way to feeling empowered, helping our child feel empowered and living the life we want them to have. However, it does require something from us. It will not fix itself. I know that with our busy schedules, it is hard to commit, and I know it's easy to get sidetracked. This is why I have made it very easy for you to get involved; in the back of the book I have enclosed letters to the board of education, the principal of your school, your state representative and others. These letters can also easily be downloaded for free from my webpage (www.bullyproofyourkidz.com). We all know the saying "the squeaky wheel gets the grease." The more people we can get involved, the better the outcome will be for our children.

*Unless someone like you cares a whole awful lot.*
*Nothing is going to get better, it is not.*
Dr. Seuss

## Chapter 2
## The evolution of a bully

My 11-year-old son has explained to me what he thinks a bully is: "I think a bully is someone that doesn't really believe in themselves, and it is their way to take the anger out on others. Sometimes someone who had to leave one school because they were bullied becomes the bully at the new school, and now it's their turn. They feel that now they can take on the role as the big bully and see how it feels. Well, that 's my opinion, anyway." I love my son.

It's a fact that most bullying takes place in middle school, and no wonder. Puberty is marked by enormous changes to the child. Adolescence is also a whirlwind of thoughts, moods and emotions that help us determine who we are. Kids have to deal with the changes that are taking place, personal discovery, the fact that their best friend might become their worst enemy the next day, the fear of not fitting in. Add to this the enormous pressure from media, from music videos to movies, from reality TV shows to the expectations from adults like: "You're a big girl/big boy now." "You don't get to do that anymore." It's a confusing time for everyone including the bully. It certainly is a confusing time as parents: our children disappearing into the virtual world of the computer/cyberspace, smiling and having fun with their friends on Skype, playing computer games with their friends from school, or their friends on the other side of the country or world for that matter. The world has changed for us all and especially for our children, and keeping them safe is harder as we face the possibility of them being bullied online maybe not more than five feet away from where we are sitting in our living room.

When we as parents think about a bully, we oftentimes picture the stereotype of someone lurking behind a tree that jumps out as you're walking home from school and beats you up, takes your backpack, and throws away your homework and your books. Sometimes you have to pay him money to get a "free pass" to walk by. We might think this is typical; however, the reality is that bullying occurs much more often at the school and in the schoolyard than on the way home from school.

For the longest time, it was also thought that bullying was just something that children had to go through, that it would "build character." However, it is now evident that bullying can have a long- lasting, harmful effect on both the victim and also the bully.

It's important to understand that not all arguments or confrontations are considered bullying. When two children approximately the same size and height are fighting or arguing, that is not bullying. Bullying is when one person who is considered more powerful finds someone that is smaller than or not as powerful as him/her and continually harasses them.

The most common form of bullying is verbal. Physical bullying is actually the least common form of bullying. Most often physical bullying tends to be amongst boys, while girl bullies often use the silent treatment. It is most common that girl bullies only girls, while boys bully both girls and boys, anyone that they feel is weaker. The weakness is not only physical; a tiny little girl with confidence can stand up to a bully, where a 5'9 4th grader with self-esteem challenges can be brutally bullied. There is no evidence that bullying is worse than it ever was, however, it is much more visible.

When I talk to children that have been bullied, I ask the question: "Why don't you tell your parents? Why are you so reluctant to report the problem?" Most of them say that they do not want to worry their parents; a lot of them say they are really worried about retaliation. Some of them feel embarrassed that they cannot stand up for themselves and deal with the problem on their own. However, the most common answer is: "Why say something? No one is going to do anything about it anyway."

We really need to change that attitude in our kids and show them that we are not bystanders, and that we really do want to make things easier for them. Before we go any further, I feel it is important to distinguish the different types of bullying. I know you have heard of them before, but a little reminder might be a good thing.

I will just briefly go over the four most common types of bullying: verbal, social, physical and cyber.

Though verbal bullying is often looked at as no big deal and ignored, it is very serious. This form of bullying can be ruthless. A person who has been verbally abused for a long time often wishes he/she was hit instead, because then he/she can show a bruise. The bruises that develop because of hurtful words take a long time to heal, and sometimes these hurts don't ever heal. There's an old children's saying: "Sticks and stones may break my bones, but words can never hurt me." It would be wonderful if that were true, but it is not. Of course words cannot break bones, but they can surely break your spirit and even your heart, and words can devastate you. The problem is that when someone hurts us, we "play the tape" over and over again in our heads. Cruel, venomous, judging words are verbal abuse; normally, verbal bullying includes teasing, name-calling, taunting, threats and inappropriate sexual comments.

Social bullying, also called relational bullying. This is when you leave someone out on purpose, tell others not to be friends with someone, spread rumors about someone, gossip, or lie about someone. This form of bullying is mostly found among girls. Often, girls take pride in being the "mean girl." They need an audience and often recruit other girls to be a part of their "circle." To be a "member," oftentimes you have to become "friends" with that month's target and collect information, which then will be used to torment the target. It is downright cruel and insensitive.

Social bullying can be used as a tool by bullies to control others or to improve the bully's social standing. Social bullying can go on for a very long time without being noticed. The goal of social bullying is to belittle and harm another individual or group. You might find children teasing an unpopular child, making fun of the way they speak, the clothes they wear, their race or culture. It's a way for those in popular groups or cliques to exclude others.

Physical bullying is when you try to hurt a person's body or possessions, which includes hitting, spitting, pushing, intimidating or trying to control another person, making mean or rude hand gestures, stealing, or forcing someone to fight or harm another person. We normally think of physical bullies as boys; however there are a lot of girls ready to fight and who threaten to hurt others. Oftentimes we ask ourselves how we can know if kids are just playing around (horseplay). During roughhousing, both children are laughing and having fun; they are not trying to physically hurt each other.

Most physical bullying peaks between grades 6-8, and after that it tapers off. Another form of physical bullying is hazing. Hazing is the use of rituals to test prospective members of a certain group. Hazing is seen in many different types of social groups: gangs, military units, schools, sports teams, fraternities and sororities. Hazing is a way for the aggressors to show that they are powerful and have power over the target. Most hazing incidents are not reported, because the target is afraid they will be excluded from the group, and often they are embarrassed about what they did to become a member. What is important here is to realize that physical bullying puts the targeted child in immediate danger, and can lead to serious problems in the form, bloody noses, scratches, broken bones or worse.

Cyber-bullying: Cyber bullying is bullying that takes place using electronic technology, such as cell phones, computers, iPads, the Internet, text messages, social media sites, chat and websites. It is the act of posting mean and hurtful comments, pictures, spreading rumors, and harassing people with the use of technology.

Unfortunately, despite all the work that has been done with anti-bullying programs and school policies, only eighteen states have cyber-bullying laws. They are: Arkansas, California, Connecticut, Florida, Hawaii, Kansas, Louisiana, Massachusetts, Missouri, Nevada, New Hampshire, North Carolina, New York, Oregon, Tennessee, Utah, Virginia and Washington. Cyber-bullying laws have been proposed in Georgia, Illinois, Kentucky, Nebraska and Maine.

Forty-nine states have bullying laws, and forty nine states have anti-bullying school policies.

In 2012, *The European Journal of Developmental Psychology* printed an article regarding cyber bullying entitled: "Cyber-bullying: An Overrated Phenomenon?" The article argues that media reports about the cyber bullying have been exaggerated. Dr. Dan Olweus of the University of Bergen, Norway, conducted a study involving students from both the USA and Norway, 450,000 students in almost 1400 schools. The students were surveyed between 2007 and 2010. The findings concluded that cyber bullying is not an epidemic as many articles and news accounts would have you believe. "The paper argues that several claims about cyber bullying made in the media and in other places are greatly exaggerated and have little factual scientific support. Opposing these claims, it proposes that cyber bullying, when studied in proper context, is a low-prevalence phenomenon, which has *not* increased over time and has *not* created many 'new' victims and bullies, that is, children and youth who are not also involved in some form of traditional bullying." As a result of these findings, Dr. Olweus recommends that bullying be addressed as a whole, without trying to separate cyber-behavior from traditional "face-to-face" bullying.

If this study holds up, as more and more people invest in cell-phones, iPads, and computers, we are again back to dealing with "basic" bullying behavior.

It might be that cyber bullying has not created "new" victims and bullies; unfortunately, it seems that cyber bullying is here to stay. Cyber bullying is anonymous and can allow anyone to bully without being identified. It has been argued that someone who has never engaged in traditional bullying might start cyber bullying.

The fact that these bullies go unnoticed and do their dirty work in the safety of anonymity is unacceptable. Of course, if it gets so bad that someone commits suicide, then it's taken seriously and everyone starts talking about implementing laws and punishment. We need to get involved and get things in place to address the problem A while ago a case that got a lot of attention was when a 13- year-old girl committed suicides after being taunted by a neighboring mom pretending to be a 16-year-old boy. The scary thing is that an adult was the perpetrator. When a parent is the bully, the home becomes a training ground for bullying behavior for their child. As long as we don't have cyber bullying laws or amendments to already existing policies, we are like bystanders watching someone being bullied. What are we waiting for? Contact your representative, and make it urgent. Only around 50% of bullies fit the profile of a person who loses his or her temper quickly, dislikes authority and thinks of violence in a positive way to get what they want. A lot of bullies have perceived "high self-esteem" and good social skills, are popular, do well in school, get along with adults and are generally happy. The sad thing is that they might not even know they are bullies. All bullies have the same motivation: to seek power over others. Most bullies use aggression as a way to achieve and maintain a popularity they feel they are entitled to. Most bullies are used to getting their own way; they are adept at recognizing and manipulating others' weaknesses.

Lately, researchers have found that a bully's behavior has more to do with his/her own feeling of shame. Psychologists have found that kids who behave like bullies, can, as we said earlier, come across as if they have high self-esteem. However, they often feel shameful about themselves, and they're scared that their shortcomings will be exposed. They are afraid that they are not "good enough," and do not meet their own expectations of what they should be. There's an unhealthy self-esteem issue here, a refusal to see anything negative in oneself. Even though one might see them as self-confident on the surface, these people have underlying insecurities regarding the way the view themselves. These insecurities, for example, can be found in their defensive characteristics, or in their grandiose view of themselves.

The very sad thing about bullies, whichever category they belong to, is their complete lack of empathy. They give themselves permission to treat someone else badly, and they feel they are above the law. More than 50% of bullying stops when a bystander steps in to make it stop. A bully does not bully only for the sake of self gratification; he bullies to be noticed, and when he notices that witnesses don't do anything, in his mind he has their vote, their agreement with his behavior. Oftentimes, the bystander is afraid to get involved because they fear they might be the next target. Bystanders do not understand their enormous power. A bully is like a pack animal: he/she does not enjoy being alone. Therefore, when bystanders stick together and state that the bully's behavior is not okay, things change rather quickly.

When we talk about bullies, we normally think of children, but bullies can be found in all sizes and shapes, amongst teachers, coaches, family members, etc. At times, they may use their position of power to intimidate, humiliate, insult, yell, or show physical aggression toward a child. I will never forget the story I was told about a little boy in 1st grade. He was sitting in the front row, and at times the teacher (who had quite a temper) would yell at the children in the class to get their attention. This little boy who came from a home where the dad yelled a lot had learned from his mom that the safe thing to do was to cover your ears; that way you did not have to hear the yelling. Anyway, covering his ears in the classroom was not appreciated by the teacher, who, instead of asking why the child was covering his ears, automatically decided he was disrespectful and told him to stand outside the classroom "until he could behave." Sometimes she sent him into the classroom next door. What she did not realize was that by not dealing with the child in a positive manner and getting to the bottom of the problem, she put a negative stamp on him, which a few of the children in the class, took as an okay to bully him at recess. It is very important that you talk to your child about how teachers and coaches make them feel and how they behave toward him/her. If you feel there's a problem, confront it. If you don't protect your child and listen to their concerns, who will?

Children with strong leadership skills can be bullies. They have lots of confidence in themselves in one area of "who they are," and are often perceived by both teachers and students as cool and popular, and they are often looked at as charming, intelligent, powerful and strong. They often get along with adults and are happy most of the time, and they might not even realize the hurtful effect they are having of their fellow students, Other times they have a very sophisticated understanding of what they are doing, are very good manipulators and are often under the impression that they are above the law, that rules are for everyone else but them. And because of their charm they expect to be able to get away with it, even though they know better. If their life is so charmed, why do they choose to bully? They bully because they need to feel more powerful, they have to protect their place in the pecking order and make sure that no one dares to challenge their place of power and status. Very often, these kids are very developed when it comes to taking advantage of other students' vulnerabilities; they are experts at turning people against each other, using gossip, rumors and other form of indirect bullying. These kids bully because they have been able to get away with it. Even teachers fall for their charm. According to Health Day, a study has shown that teens who are trying to remain well-liked by their peers are more likely to bully other kids.

It is a choice to be bully; it is a very bad choice, but nevertheless a choice.

Things the bully would not want you to know are that they really are having a hard time communicating their feelings and their needs. Oftentimes they themselves do not know what is missing. They think that other children admire them for being bullies because they dare to do things that are against the rules, and they are under the impression that their friends will admire them more if they continue to bully. Sometimes they want other children to hurt because they hurt inside. They will do anything to avoid the exposure of their short comings. A bully is a child that is trying to fit in like everyone else, but they are willing to do whatever it takes and have no empathy for others.

Oftentimes they will argue that they are just "assertive," that they are not "aggressive." What they are doing is hiding that they are inept and weak in so many ways, and a way for them to hide their inadequateness is to bully someone. What some people mistakenly see as psychological strength is someone showing their determination to hurt and violate other people, someone with no care or consideration for others, no care for anyone's boundaries, and little thought of the consequences of their choice to bully. When caught, they will try make an excuse and try to put a socially acceptable face on their very unacceptable behavior. Most all states has anti bullying laws, and the bully knows they might get caught, but bullying is like a drug to them, and most need to be taught how to stop. Statistics show that if a bully in school is *not* confronted by teachers, and if parents do not intervene, the bully will likely have a criminal record by the age of 24. They also have a higher risk of physical health problems, increased risk of depression, addiction and suicide when they grow up. So by making a choice to torment others, the bully condemns himself to a lifelong pattern of aggression and a failure to grow out of it, which can have very serious consequences.

So the evolution of the bully continues, with more avenues for bullying available to them than ever before. We can make a difference by getting educated and being aware. However, it is of utmost importance to listen to our children and bring them around to opening up. We have to help them understand that they are not responsible for our happiness, and they do not have to protect us by not letting us know what is going on. There's an amazing opportunity for developing closeness and a feeling of safety with our children when we do this.

*No one has yet fully realized the wealth of sympathy, kindness and*
*generosity hidden in the soul of a child.*
*The effort of every true education should be*
*to unlock that treasure.*
Emma Goldman

## Chapter 3
## Stereotyping, cultural differences and working it out

Stereotyping is "to believe unfairly that all people or things with a particular characteristic are the same."

Racial remarks, sexual remarks, and gender remarks are the most common behaviors based on stereotypes, but stereotypes based on social group membership can be just as damaging, such as "jocks" picking on "geeks." Stereotyping, like hazing, is generally accepted worldwide.

The United States is now more diverse than it has ever been, however, I feel that when you watch movies or TV shows, you notice soon that most actors of color seems to play stereo typical roles, such as immigrants, maids, and criminals. At times when they do have a leading role, it seems that the character always has a really bad past, horrible childhood and a chip on his/her shoulder, which makes him/her feel that he/she has to prove to the world that he/she is "worthy."

One of the best movies on the subject of stereotyping and sticking to one's own clique is the 1985 movie *The Breakfast Club*. In this movie, five students, the "criminal," the "jock," the "brain," the "basket case" and the "princess" report for Saturday morning detention. From there the kids realize that even thought they appear different at first, they are all faced with similar struggles. This movie is a in many circles considered a classic. It offers quite an insight into the problem of stereotyping.

One thing to keep in mind is that at times stereo typing is not done to be unkind; at times people do not even think they are stereo typing. They might even think they are complimenting you. When someone just assumes you are awesome in sports just because you are African American, or super good in school because you are Asian, they are putting a label and possibly a lot of strain on you, and even though they might not have intended to be insensitive or even hurt you, they often times do.

In times like this, we are dealing with beliefs that are part of our society. However, instead of ignoring it and possibly letting it ruin your day, in a pleasant voice say something like, "Thank you for the compliment, however, I'm not interested in sports. My passion is reading." Being truthful and informative without attitude and anger will make it better for both sides.

Other times, stereotypical comments and behaviors are not innocent. At times, they are meant to be derogatory and done to intentionally hurt someone who is different. This kind of behavior commonly accompanies bullying.

Many of us witnessed the evolution of stereotyping of a group of people in the USA after 9/11. If you were from or looked like you were from the Middle East after September 11th , 2001, you would have noticed a shift in people's attitude. Our country was in a state of fear, anger and distress. We were all scared. At this time, the stereotyping of someone from the Middle East, or someone who looked as if they were from the Middle East, hit a high. Of course in our hearts we knew that most Middle Easterners weren't terrorists, but fear made most of the population put common sense on the shelf and we went into survival mode. Everyone needs to feel safe and the fear of another terrorist attack was something many Americans felt. The FBI reported a 1700% increase in hate crimes towards American Muslims in the years that followed September 11th. It certainly did not make matters any better when we felt that the Muslim community did not speak up. In her book *Living Hell*, Ghazal Omid (a human rights and women's rights advocate) explained the silence like this: "Nothing we do seems to be right. If we don't speak up, we are considered passive. If we do speak up, we receive hate mail and death threats, we are told you are on your own. Give us media attention so we can tell our side and we can help fight the terrorists. Don't give terrorists all the attention." If we allow fear, the biggest internal bully of all, to run our lives, we will continue to feel anxiety and stress, feelings that work against our choice to learn, understand and give diversity a chance.

The sad thing about stereotyping is that growing up believing that stereotypes are for real, we continue to live in the state of ignorance; and should we choose to teach our children the same nonsense, the unhealthy circle continues.

When you think about it, why do we make the choice to stereotype? I believe that when we do not completely understand who someone is, what they stand for or where they come from (oftentimes we might not even care to do the research to get to know them), we give ourselves the permission to fill in the blanks. If we also have been watching the media, we might already have decided who this person is before they even open their mouth; it is interesting because then what we choose to do is to discriminate against someone without any facts to back us up. I am not saying that there is something wrong with pointing out our real differences, whether they are cultural, religious, or anything else. What I am saying is that when one makes choices to be rude, demeaning, elitist or arrogant in our behavior we need to stop.

When we celebrate our differences, take responsibility for our own actions, teach our children respect and integrity, explain to our children that stereotyping is nothing more than an illusion, that it is not real and that it is bullying, I believe our children will grow up making the right decisions. I believe that they are what we teach them. You might tell yourself that you do not want your child to play with or hang out with someone different than you and your family, and that is your choice, but I do believe that if you do so, you are missing out on a great opportunity for growth. Change is the one thing you can count on. America and the rest of the world is changing, and it is up to us as individuals to make sure the change is for the good, and that can come only from the individual (yes, you!). Make it a goal to teach acceptance and kindness towards all.

Steve Jobs once said: "The one who are crazy enough to think they can change the world are the ones who do." Be one of the ones willing to make a difference, be it in small ways around you and your family, or in a large way. I truly believe that when we start teaching acceptance to our children and when we, as parents, grandparents, aunts and uncles embrace it, the big change will come. A concept of diversity shaping our world, bringing to light cultural awareness.

We all know that the United States is a melting pot of different cultures, an exciting country that people dream of coming to. After the 2010 census was taken, the percentage of people living in the USA was divided as follow: 63% white, 16.5% Hispanic, 12.5% African American, 4,7% Asian, .7% American Indian & Alaskan, .15% Hawaiian, and 2.45% other races. A lot of different cultures to celebrate; an opportunity for education and learning.

Making choices to learn about different cultures is a gift you can give to your children, and to yourself for that matter. I feel that it is only by making an effort to learn and appreciate difference that we can move away from internal fear (which can come out in the form of bullying) and move in the direction of acceptance. Personally, learning about different cultures has always fascinated me, and being able to develop friendship with children all over the world started for me at the young age of ten in the form of having pen pals. The friendships I made have grown so strong over the years that a few weeks ago I had lunch with my pen pal from Switzerland, who was visiting the US, and dinner with my pen pal from Hawaii, all in one week. For my

18th birthday, my friend in India sent me a sari, the dress worn by many Indian women; it was fun for us Norwegian girls to try to put it on. At the same time, my friends in Malaysia, Japan, Australia, South Africa, the United States, etc. were learning about Norway and what we are all about.

There are some things that I have learned from my pen pals over the years that might also help you to get a short glimpse into why sometimes things can seem so confusing. Here are just a few examples: did you know that in the Middle East, the interests and decisions of the "we" (the group) are more important than "I"? That kind of thinking is considered a "relationship culture."... It's also about the family honor and saving face. Saying no can be very difficult for someone from that part of the world. Instead of answering a question with a direct "no," the person might try to answer in a way so that it is easier to save face. They might say, "I will try," or "I might consider that." Insults or criticism are taken very seriously. The father has the last word in all decisions surrounding the family and religion is the center of all things. This culture has a completely different approach to time than us, a much slower pace. Age and wisdom are honored and so is wealth. For us Westerners, it can be hard for us to understand that "we" take precedence over "I." We are such an individual-based society; honor and shame are important, but not that important in our culture. For us, religion is very individual and not talked about much. However, we are very structured when it comes to time, and deadlines must be met. Just these few cultural differences could make room for serious conflict if we are not aware of them and take them into consideration when we are communicating, it could get awkward for both parties.

I remember once one of my Indian friends asked me to hand her a pair of scissors. I handed them over and she did not take them. I asked if she wanted them and she said: "Please put them down. In my culture, we do not touch a scissor, knife or anything that can be considered a weapon at the same time as someone else, because that is not good for our friendship." I learned something that day.

Books could be written (and probably are) on the subject of the differences in cultures. I'm going to spend a few more minutes on a few more cultural differences. My hope is that it will be helpful to you and that you might learn something new, or remind yourself of something you might have forgotten. In doing so, I hope to bring more understanding to "different."

In the United States, it is considered rude to show up late for dinner. If you are going to be later than fifteen minutes, you should call. However, in Argentina and other South American places it is rude to be on time. In Japan, Norway and many other countries, it is rude to walk into someone's home with your shoes on. Why would you want to bring sand and dirt into someone's home? In the United States, we politely ask someone "How are you." The answer we are looking for is "fine," "great" and we might add a "thank you." In other cultures, it seems strange to ask someone how they are unless you really want to know the answer. In Scandinavian countries, you would only ask this question to someone you know well and who you intend to have a conversation with. In some countries, it is considered polite to leave a little bit of food on your plate; this shows that you got enough to eat. In many cultures, pointing is considered rude. You would instead use an open hand as a way and never point with one finger. In America, we respect our "comfort zone" (personal space). Chinese, on the other hand, do not have a lot of distance in their comfort zone, and if you move away, they might follow. In China, it is common to applaud. If someone applauds for you, you are expected to applaud back. The list goes on and on, and it is understandable that conflict and confusion takes place. That's also why we can be proactive and teach our children about different cultures, and that's why you should consider going into your child's classroom and sharing things about your culture. Teachers are always open and appreciate your involvement.

One of the fun things about teaching children to recognize differences in people, as well as teaching them how we are similar, is that when children understand that people can be different and unique, but that we still have a lot in common, it makes them more open to developing respect and acceptance for others.

A fun thing to do on a school field trip would be to go and observe cultural events where children can learn to accept differences and also notice similarities among people; it gives them an opportunity to learn and to get along with others much better. When they understand someone else's viewpoint and uniqueness, they will hopefully choose to be better at developing their own cooperation skills. In doing so, they will boost their self-esteem, because they will recognize and accept who they are, and feel good about themselves as other children recognize the worth of their traditions or who they are. As we encourage children to ask question that help them understand more about others being different than them, we validate that it's okay to be different.

When I arrived in the United States, I made a choice to first be a guest in this country and then make it my home. As emigrants to this beautiful country, we need to take the responsibility to teach our children about our own culture, and then leave the history of the United States to schools and teachers. We as parents must make an effort to honor what America is all about and why we want to live here. We might ask questions like: What makes you proud to live in the United States?   What are the things that show that you are an American? These are questions that will make your child look at this country with more of a feeling of belonging. Coming from you, the parent, it will have a great impact on your child, especially when they see the gratitude and passion you have for your new homeland.

As far as gender stereotyping, I feel that when we teach our children to look at each other as individuals first rather than as our genders, gender stereotyping does not become an issue. It is more and more common to see both boys and girls being invited to birthday parties, instead of only girls to a girl's party and vice versa. Children are playing together on the playground as individuals; they are having fun playing a variety of activities and new games, and not only gender-accepted games. Even so, you might still hear a child say, "stupid girl" or "stupid boy." This would be the time to suggest for them to express themselves using a statement that makes it clear that they are angry at someone, not necessarily the gender of who they are mad at. We learn this harmful stereotypical attitude at an early age from observing the different roles people in our own families play. As we grow older, the stereotype might be reinforced by friends, family, movies, video games, etc., or even to a degree supported by an unspoken bias from our educational system. The reality is that both boys and girls are more alike than they are different. They have the same goals of wanting self-fulfillment, being accepted for who they are, friends, love, affection, and achievement; they want to be acknowledged first as a unique individual, then after that as boys or girls. As we teach our children acceptance, respect and getting along, we are working on diminishing stereotyping and this could play a big role in getting the ugly issue of bullying under control.

*Instead of being presented with stereotypes by age, sex,*
*color, class or religion, children must have the opportunity*
*to learn that within each range, some people are*
*loathsome and some are delightful.*
Margaret Mead

# Chapter 4
## Seven ways to help your child handle bullies

**1. Self respect and self-esteem. When your child has feelings of self worth, they are less likely to be bullied.**

The most important gift you can give your child is the gift of understanding and practicing self worth. Feelings of self worth are the building blocks of a child's well being. We as parents are the main source of our children's opinion of themselves.

There is a big difference between teaching healthy self worth and turning your child into someone who truly believes they can do nothing wrong and constantly points the finger at someone else. As my grandma always said: "When you point one finger at someone else, three fingers point at you." Teaching children to respect others is as important as teaching them about their worth. If a child constantly feels like a loser and doesn't believe in themselves, they have a much higher chance of being bullied. You are the one setting the standard of what your child is willing to accept as far as how people treat them. If you treat them with respect, then that is what they expect from other people too. If you baby them and do not allow them to grow up age appropriately, they feel like an outsider and have challenges with communicating with their peers. If you raise your child in a bubble, they are in for hard lessons in the real world. On the other hand, allowing them early on to have unsupervised access to the Internet, movies, magazines, etc. and allowing them to grow up too fast is as big a problem. A young child cannot comprehend grown up humor or movies; they can be confusing and taken completely out of context. There is always a middle ground.

To have self-esteem, they also must have self control. This is very important, as having the child lose control and have an outburst is one of the things that "feed" the bully. Teach your child self control by encouraging them to walk away from frustrating situations instead of having an outburst, as well as teaching them to evaluate what it is that causes them to lose control and then try to make sense of their own feelings. The best thing to do in dealing with frustration is to THINK before responding to a situation. Always encourage your child to talk about their feelings, which does not mean that they interrupt every time they need to say something and you stop what you are doing and focus only on him/her. This child turns into a little brat. Tell them you would love to hear what they have to say, and agree to a time when you will get back to him/her. When you give your child positive feedback, it teaches them to think good thoughts about themselves.

It is important to speak to your child with respect and kindness and always make sure they understand the difference between their behavior and their character. When you reprimand them, always make sure it is their behavior you do not like; it is not them as a person. It is important that you help your child set realistic expectations. If they expect to be number one at everything they do, they will have a really hard time when that does not happen.

When you teach your child to understand that the person he/she sees in the mirror is amazing, it makes them feel good inside and starts to develop feelings of being comfortable with themselves, someone worthy of love and respect. Of course, we do not want to raise small, arrogant narcissists; like everything else in life, it needs balance. It means that we teach them a realistic understanding of how they have some great strengths, and like everyone else they have some areas that need working on. Always encourage any talent your child has. It might not be what you are fond of, but for him/her it's something they fell really great about. When we encourage them in their talents, it makes them want to succeed in other aspects of life too.

No parent or child can have a smile on their face all the time, but when you as a parent are unhappy, it transfers to your children. If you try to put on a happy face, they see through that immediately. So be honest, tell them if you are having a bad day, but that it is not because of them. Always make sure you tell them they are fun to be with, that their behavior pleases you, that what they think and their opinions are important to you. It does not mean that because you listen to their opinion they are going to get everything they want.

Make sure your child feels safe in expressing him/herself. If you never allow your child to express their feelings, never give them a time to express themselves, they start to close up and not feel that what they are feeling is important to anyone.

**2. Teach them the difference between aggressive and assertive.**

When you teach your child to be assertive, you teach them that they are allowed to express their own ideas, opinions, and talents. They will learn the value of being positive and honest and will stand up to someone in a non-aggressive way. Assertive children are not likely to allow other children to influence them to do something they feel is wrong or may lead them into trouble. They think for themselves and do not just follow others. They question ideas and tell the truth about what they think is fair, and they will at times do that to an adult too. You really have to emphasize the importance that, even though they are being assertive, that does not mean they always will get their own way. Again, we must teach them to respect and honor other people, and respect that others might have a different opinion than they do.

When you talk to your child about being assertive, it is also important to teach them self control. A lot of children act without thinking, and then they deal with the consequences later on. When you know how you feel, you are much more able to evaluate and make the right decisions before you act. Being aggressive is an incorrect and immature way of problem solving, relating to others and getting what you want. Aggressive people are often demanding and selfish; they love to create conflict and stress.

I decided to use a game to show my son a way to differentiate between aggressive and assertive. I took a clear water glass and put it on the table. I then took a few of his Star Wars figures and put them on the table next to the glass. I told him to throw a ball onto the figurines, and of course they all fell down. I then took the figurines and put them into the glass, and told him to throw the ball, and of course nothing happened; the figurines were standing tall. I explained to him that this is true with both aggressive behavior and aggressive words. When we have our shield up (the water glass in this example), nothing can hurt us. So when we experience aggressive behavior and we have the shield of assertiveness around us, nothing anyone says or does can hurt us.

I remember one time my son was about five years old. I had just picked him up from school and we were walking back to my car when we happened to walk by the playground where a little girl was riding around on her tricycle. She looked at Branden and asked him: "What's wrong with your face?" Branden, in a very self-assured way, said: "There is nothing wrong with my face; I have a scar from having had surgery when I was little. I was born with a cleft palate and cleft lip, and the doctors had to fix it." The little girl said, "Oh" and continued to ride her bike. Because Branden was not intimidated, he felt free to simply educate the girl, and all was well. I was very proud of my son for the way he handled that situation at such a young age.

## 3. Teach your child to set boundaries.

Boundaries send clear messages: A physical boundary empowers kids to identify and create their own safe spaces: This is my space, don't come any further. At the same time, they learn to respect the personal space of others. Emotional boundaries teach them that it is not okay to say hurtful things to others or to bully someone. Helping children set boundaries is healthy and will help to set them up for success in relationships throughout their lives. The best way to teach children about healthy boundaries is for parents to have healthy boundaries themselves and to model them. Showing respect for others, making sure that everyone in your home has a right to their own feelings and space, and honesty, even about any challenges you might have, are important aspects of this. Sometimes children are so concerned about fitting in that they will allow someone to treat them badly, as long as they allow them to hang out with them. When your child asks you to allow them to, for example, give away their favorite Lego in trade for being invited over to their "friend's" house, it is time to talk about choices and boundaries.

## 4. Role play at home.

One of the best ways to teach your child how to deal with bullies and bullying situations is role playing at home. This can actually turn into something really funny, so use humor wherever you can. It is important that you understand your child's situation; you might think you know their personality, but they can at times be very different at school than at home. Make sure you familiarize yourself with your child's individual personality and also make sure they are comfortable with your suggestions. If you role play something they do not feel comfortable with or would never do, it is not very helpful. However, when you suggest something they feel good about, they will feel so much better and be ready to take it on.

Teach them how they can get their point across to their peers, an adult, and their teachers and explain how they feel. Give them ideas on how to approach a teacher to explain what is going on. Make sure you understand exactly where the bullying is taking place: is it at school, on the bus, or in the hall way? Discuss different approaches with your child and set the stage. There is no place better for helping your child with these issues than your own home. Home is where they are safe and where we can teach them about the real world.

**5. Communicating and telling the truth.**

It is common for children to at times lie. When they are very young, they do not understand the difference between what is truth and what is not. They will tell you that their unicorn told them they should get a chocolate; they are innocent and use fantasy to tell their story. After preschool, they start to lie in an attempt to hide things they know they should not have done. They are embarrassed and are afraid of the consequences they expect they will get from the adult. Sometimes children with low self-esteem can brag or inflate their stories to impress others, often to be accepted and be cool.

Never call your child a liar; when you put a negative "mark" on your child like that, it ruins their self-esteem and leads to negative self talk. Let bygones be bygones. Don't bring up things from the past, e.g. "This is just who you are," or "You always lie." Don't set "traps" for your child to catch them in a lie. If you know they did not make their bed, why ask them if they did? You are inviting them to lie. Simply say: "When I check your room in five minutes, I expect to see the bed already made." Explain to your child why lying is not a good thing to do. Tell the story about the boy who cried wolf. They might not understand that, if they continue to lie, people will not believe them even when they are telling the truth. So if they go to a teacher and tell them that so and so bullied them, and they are known to be someone who lies, will the teacher believe them?

If you catch your child in a blatant lie, tell him/her you know he/she is telling a lie. Tell them it is normal to be uncomfortable with the thought of the consequences for telling a lie. Ask them if they feel it is a good choice to lie. Tell them lying is never helpful, and ask, "What do you suggest we do together to make it easier for you to always be truthful?"

I remember when my son was five years old, he was out in the garage, and he had climbed on a five- gallon paint bucket. It tipped over and he spilled the whole thing, I was inside and had no idea. We were having lunch when he said to me: "Mom, you know how you told me that I should always be honest with you and always tell the truth? And if I am, you will not give me a time out; we will talk about it instead?" I said yes, and he said, "Well, you might not like what happened in the garage this morning. I accidently climbed on a big paint can and it fell over, and someone must not have put the lid on really good because the paint is all over the floor." Man, was it a mess to clean up. The stains are still visible on my floor. But I was proud of him for telling the truth.

Make sure your child understands how important it is for them to take responsibility. I explained it to my son this way: "When you take responsibility, it makes you powerful. You do not give your power away, you get to keep it." Of course, make sure you praise them for telling the truth, and explain to them how proud you are of them; also explain to them that the consequences will be easier when they tell the truth before you figure it out on your own.

**6. Teach children about the danger of cyber space.**

Technology is everywhere: Personal computers, iPads, smart phones, chat rooms, online games, etc. Always make sure you keep the computer in a place where it is easy for you to oversee, and make sure you use privacy settings and parental controls. (This is a must, even on gaming devices.) Make sure you check the browsing history too. Make sure you have all of your child's passwords, screen names and profiles, and check the privacy settings for any application or website they use. Work with your child online together. Set guidelines about who they can have as friends online, and check their friend list. If there's a name you do not know, have your child tell you about who the person is and how they met them. Always make your child understand that you are doing this for their safety and that you are the adult.

Check their password from time to time. If they have changed it without your knowledge, make the consequences be less time on the Internet, with the opportunity for them to earn back their Internet time. Go to Google and Google your child's name. Do it both in the search engine and under images. Make sure you check up on any online use that seems secretive. When you walk up on them and they change the screen, you know something is up. Make sure you explain the importance of never giving out phone numbers, addresses, or any other personal information. Also, make sure they understand that they should never give out password, their screen name, etc. Talk to your child about your concerns and make sure you limit your child's exposure to sites where people can easily behave anonymously. With message choices like Confide, Sneaky, Secret and Whisper, users are able to send anonymous messages or images to anyone who use this kind of app. The apps are so "smart" that some of them "self destruct" after the message has been delivered, making it impossible to figure out who sent the message, bullied you, etc.

Talk to your children's school about how they protect the children from potential dangers of Internet usage. Statistics show that children who are bullied at school oftentimes are bullied on the Internet too.

**7. Educate your child on showing forgiveness and empathy, even to a bully.**

The difference between sympathy and empathy is that in empathy you are feeling with the person, "walking in someone else's shoes," and have a good sense of how they feel. When you feel sympathy, you feel *for* the person; you're sorry for them, but you do not understand what they are feeling.

My friend Pat once told me: Forgiveness does not mean re-unification.

We have heard many times that holding on to resentment is like taking poison and expecting the other person to die. Know that forgiveness doesn't suggest that you condone whatever painful thing happened to you, and it has nothing to do with admitting defeat or being stepped on. It's about giving you the power of feeling happiness NOW. The thought of forgiving someone who has hurt you seems strange, and the most common thing for humans is to want revenge, but letting go and moving forward needs to be our goal. That you forgive someone does not mean that you are now best friends.

One of the most powerful ways to teach children empathy is to be empathetic ourselves in the way we parent our children. When your child does something you do not approve off, do not yell, scream or hit. This teaches your child that yelling and hitting is an acceptable way to show our feelings. As our children get older, they can learn empathy from how we treat them. Show interest in their stories, listen to them when they talk, and help them understand their own feelings and thoughts by asking questions. As they grow and their empathy grows because of how we model it to them, they will be more willing to help others, show generosity and lend a helping hand. A child that cares for others, encourages others, and is always there to give a helping hand makes life easier for others as well as for themselves.

Remember, when a child is able to feel indifferent about a bully, he/she has arrived in the place of "I matter" and it can give them a feeling of being powerful.

*Education is the most powerful weapon which can be used to change the world.*
Nelson Mandela

# Chapter 5
## Trust in yourself and your parental instincts, and get involved

You might be thinking to yourself, "What does trusting myself have to do with bullying?" Well, it has a lot to do with it. Bullying is not a surface problem; it goes deep into the psyche of both the child and parent. There's a reason why some children act out and others behave in a healthy way. I believe that the more we open up to ourselves and look inward, the more help we can be to our children.

When we bring home our little bundle of love, our beautiful little baby, wouldn't it be nice if he/she came with an instruction manual, a blueprint for success? I believe all of us have a built in feeling of what we should and should not do (our gut instinct). Our problem is so often that we do not trust ourselves; we question our own decisions and often go with the advice of others. Often, they seem so sure of themselves, and of course they are; they are giving you advice. It does not affect them, so it is easy to tell you what to do. Trust in your own gut, refer to it often, and check in with yourself, because the more you trust yourself, the more strength you will have available to deal with life's challenges. Do the best you can, and don't talk negatively to yourself. Be your own best friend. Don't be the kind of person who dwells on your worries and forgets your successes. You are teaching your little ones to be patient with themselves; let it also apply to you.

The better you feel about yourself, the better a parent you will be. You are the mirror for your child. Being patient is something that seems to have been "retired." Instant gratification is what we want, and we are not easy on ourselves; we get frustrated, and at times find it hard to forgive ourselves. But you know what? We are pretty darn special all in our own way. No one knows our story, and until we walk in the other person's shoes and understand how they feel, we should focus inward. Parents of both bullies and victims are living their own stories; they are trying to do the best they know how to. We might not agree with how they are living their life, still, they are doing things their way. The only person we have any power over is ourselves.

My friends and family know that one of my favorite things to do is to travel. One day I was talking to my sister about some travels I was planning, and she said, "The most amazing journey you will ever take is the journey within yourself." She is right; it is an amazing journey. I have been around people who would sleep with the TV on or a radio just to hear noise around them. They did not want to have to focus on their own thoughts, so it was better to let the mind stay busy with whatever they could feed it. If you feel this way, please consider something else; you are worthy of getting to know. Take a trip inwards. When your child sees you stopping and taking time for you, so will they. If you have questions and worries right now, such as worries about your child being bullied, or worries about the future, remember that new worries will be there down the road too, maybe in another capacity. Always remember that down the road there will be answers too, good answers, and useful solutions. Just trust and let go.

Most of us realize that our reality is only a small piece of a much bigger picture, however, we view our life through a small lens, and we make sense of our world through it. Put your thumb and your index finger together and look through the gap. You do not see a lot, do you? Yes, there is a lot we miss, and the problem is that when we and our little ones think we can transform situations into the way we want the outcome to be, we are in for a big surprise. The wonderful thing is that when we work on trying to modify our thoughts and have an open mind instead of being so set on how things "should be," we enjoy our lives more. When we remove ourselves from our one-sided reality and try to learn as much as possible about other people and places and how they perceive the world, and how we can all fit together, we start using our gift of common sense. Sometimes when we look at our decisions, we should ask ourselves if they are practical, logical and what the consequences will be if things go wrong.

I'm not suggesting you never ask for an opinion or get another perspective on something; it is great to have someone to run your ideas by. However, I'm suggesting that you do not make it your norm. Rather, trust in yourself. Sometimes we can't see the forest for the trees. It is of course important to practice being flexible and open minded and to listen to other people's ideas, even if it scares you, but just don't ignore your own thoughts. Your child will see this in you and wants to copy you. Imagine them starting this journey at a very young age, and the freedom they will have. They will be completely in tune with the fact that is okay to be whoever they are supposed to be. This will help them so much with their self-esteem. You will help your child to acknowledge and accept that they are one of a kind, someone unique, and someone worthy of listening to.

Remember to always perceive yourself and others in a positive manner. Always find the best in yourself and others. You might not be the best in everything; no one is. But you are awesome, you have your talents, and only you can release them. Like I have said before, we were born a masterpiece. Don't be in such a hurry to allow others or by your own actions turn the masterpiece into a carbon copy. Make it a conscious decision about what you will allow yourself to be influenced by and what is worthy devoting your cherished time to. It is your decision who you will allow to influence your thinking, so trust in yourself and your abilities, and allow yourself to grow and learn. And realize that the only one you can control, no matter how hard you try, is yourself.

If you were to take account of, say, the last month, the things you were busy at, the hours of "doing," how much of that time would you be excited about and wanting to do over again? I'm not talking about work here; hopefully your work and your personal life are balanced. I'm talking about your free time. Are you following your passion, and are you encouraging your little one to follow their passion? Is there room for both parents and child to enjoy their separate passions if they're not the same? Or are you feeling like a taxi driver? It is very important that you get to do things for you too. However, if you are truly and completely content and happy just doing what your child wants, than that is your choice. If, on the other hand, you really feel like you need "you time," realize that is okay and there is no reason to feel guilty about that. Your child will understand that even grownups need fun time for only them. Because the reality is that the structure and schedules you are putting on yourself could be unintentionally creating chaos in your life. We can admit it or not, but the attitude we show to our children is the guide they use to form their life, be that as a bully, victim or bystander. We have this one adventure called life, so let's enjoy it! Empower yourself, realize you are awesome, and trust in yourself!

When you have come to the place of letting go, trusting in your own instincts, it is much easier for you to be involved and see clearly what you have to do when your child is having a hard time. You cannot force or demand an outcome, and if you do, and it is short-lived. Getting what you want and protecting your child means you have to "step outside" and look into the issue at hand, and only then decide when it is appropriate for you to get involved and take matters into your own hands. By being solution- oriented and keeping an open mind as to the outcome, you can make things better. You will never get all that you want; you will have to compromise like everyone else, but you will have made an improvement, no matter what difficult situation you are facing.

If the bullying in your child's life continues and is NOT short-lived, you must get involved. If you feel that teachers and the principal at your child's school just plain do nothing, even after having been confronted about the issue, get involved. Your child might even ask you to get involved because they are having such a hard time at school. Don't blow it off. Get involved. If you hear from your child or someone else that your child has been threatened, get involved. However, it is very important that you do not go off and take care of it behind your child's back. You must invite him/her into the solution process. He/she will be the one going back to school and facing the bully.

It is important that you know everything that has been going on. Has he/she talked to the teacher? What was the outcome? Make sure you don't jump onto the bandwagon of blame before you have all the details. You might consider asking yourself, "Is my child in any way contributing to this problem?" Make sure your child knows that a bully loves to see someone's reaction. Thank your child for letting you know and reassure him/her that you will work through this together, and make sure you start keeping a written record of what has happened. If there's an injury, make sure you take a picture of it and report it to the school.

It is really important that the child knows that it is not okay to retaliate, and make sure your child avoids the bully whenever possible. Let your child know that it is normal to feel sad, hurt, embarrassed and angry. Your child needs to know that no one deserves to be bullied, and that it is not okay. However, never promise your child that you will not tell anyone. Tell him/her that you will do the best you can to not make things worse, but that it is not okay to say nothing. Do not be too quick to blame anyone, and don't jump to conclusions before you have the whole story. Suggest to the teacher/ principal that there be a meeting between you, the teacher and the principal to discuss your child's situation. Again, keep records and make sure you write down what took place, and also get the teacher's take on it. Talk to the principal and make sure you fully understand their anti-bullying policy, if they have one. Almost every state has a school anti bullying law. After you have discussed the problem with the principal and you feel it is time to have a face-to-face meeting with the parent of the bully, suggest this to the principal and ask him/her to arrange for this meeting to take place at the school.

When the meeting is set, arrive to the meeting with your goal and objective very clear. It is hard to keep it together and act civilly when your child is being attacked. However, remember that when you do meet the parents of your child's worst nightmare, the bully, that you need to speak with a non-accusatory and calm voice. Remember that they might not be aware that this is happening, so try to be understanding, and see if you can put yourself in their shoes. Because if you are defensive and send out your message in anger, a message that says: "You will hear what I have to say, and I am right and you are wrong," you will be talking to a wall.

You could consider starting by saying some nice things about their child; every child has something positive about them, even if you feel that the only thing is their haircut and their shoes. Then explain your concerns. Make sure they understand that it is how you feel. Say something like, "I'm concerned because Susie came home the other day and her backpack was ripped." Do not say, "Susie came home and your kid ripped her back pack." If you do, they will immediately be ready to defend and argue. Instead, try to explain how your daughter/son is telling you that the bullying occurs. When you have explained what you feel and how it makes your child feel, try to reach out to them and ask them if they would work with you on how things could be worked out to the benefit of both children. Allow them to express what they see. If they feel their child did it as a joke, silly child's play, or whatever, ask them to consider your viewpoint. Most of the time, the embarrassment of even being talked to about this will make them co-operate. This is not a contest where there's only one winner; this is about both parties compromising. What matters is that your child will hopefully be in a better place because of your intervention.

As I said earlier, for most parents whose child been accused of being a bully, it is embarrassing because their first thought is that you are blaming them for being bad parents. They will arrive to the meeting, ready to find a way for them or their child not to have done anything wrong. Be prepared to arrive at the table with the understanding that you have to break down the wall, and be very much aware that you will have to be the one doing most of the talking. You have to be the problem solver, and even if you feel that it did not get you anywhere and that you were talking to a wall, know you made a difference.

People will put on a lot of different acts to save face, so be persistent with what you are asking for and I believe you will see a change. Always use phrases like: "I feel…" No one can argue with how you feel. Your motivation to deal with the challenge at hand this way is for you to make sure they hear what you have to say. If you can get them to understand your point of view, you are more likely to be able to have a meaningful resolution to the problem. When you focus on your feelings instead of their child's behavior, they are more likely to empathize with your situation, listen to what you have to say, and discuss the problem in a constructive way. In this way, you have greater potential for coming up with a resolution and preventing future conflicts. Of course, it is much easier to get angry and want to give them a piece of your mind, but doing so rarely leads to positive, solution- oriented outcome.

If you say to yourself right now, "I have tried all that. Now what?" Well, you do have a few less comfortable options. First, you can go directly to the school board. Request some time at their next meeting. Be prepared and bring all your notes. Second, you could change schools. This is a very hard choice to make, but it could be best for your child. The last resort, in my opinion, is to call the local police. If your child has scrapes and bruises, you could contact the police and ask them to put a restraining order on the bully. The police could check to see if the bully already has a juvenile record. If not, you filing this claim could make it their first introduction to the juvenile system. This is a step that has to be seriously considered! Yes, your child might possibly be safer for a while, or it could backfire, and your child could be put in a place where the other children back off because they do not have knowledge of everything that went on. Even a bully gets sympathy when or if the other students feel he/she was not treated fairly. Always remember that the other children might or might not have seen what took place.

As we have talked about earlier, it is of the outmost importance that we as parents take a stand, get involved, stay in touch with the school, contact our state representatives, and make sure they are aware of what we expect them to do in the job we elected them to: protect our children. If we do not get involved and just leave it up to bureaucrats, we could end up with laws that some might consider being on the verge of taking away our freedom of speech. An example of pretty strong cyber bullying policies can be found in the Nova Scotia cyber bullying law in Canada. This law will allow anyone who feels they are being harassed on the web to be able to seek a restraining order, sue on the behalf of themselves or their child, and make the bully's parents responsible for their child's actions on the web or via cell phone if the perpetrator is under age of eighteen. New Zealand's anti bullying policy states that should any form of communication device be used to cause harm, it is punishable with up to three months in jail and a $2000 fine, and anyone over the age of fourteen can be prosecuted.

*In the game of life, we all receive a set of variables and limitations in the field of play. We can either focus on the lack thereof or empower ourselves to create better realities with the pieces we play the game with.*

T.F. Hodge

## Chapter 6
## It's not easy being different,
## but it is boring to be the same

Fighting against bullying and working with children to accept each other is very close to my heart. My son was born with a cleft palate and a cleft lip; this of course made him different, but still the most perfect little guy I had ever seen. As my son was growing up, I noticed that there were quite a few curious looks due to his scar and sometimes his speech. My son was always an active little guy and kept busy all the time. He was pretty easygoing, and as he was very young, he never really knew something was different. It was not until he started school that he realized he had something the other kids did not have. Friends, family and teachers were all very aware of the situation and kept an eye open for bullying, while also reassuring Branden (my son) that he was perfect just the way he was.

There were times he came home crying, saying, "God, why did this have to happen to me, why was I born this way?" This happened more and more as he grew older. I made a nice sign that I glued on the ceiling above his bed. On this sign I wrote "I'm a Winner," and every night before he went to sleep he would read it, and when he woke up in the morning he would read it. We also decided to have an app installed on my smart phone, which every morning would give us a positive quote. We talked about never using negative self-talk, and after a while, he started to say things like, "There are not a lot of kids my age that have gone through what I have gone through." I would agree with him and say, no there are not a lot of kids that have had your experience. He started to realize that, yes, he was different, but he started to see that if you embraced it instead of hating it, it could be a good thing.

I'm not saying that there aren't times when he gets frustrated, but he has more tools to help him overcome it. A big plus for him is also the school he goes to now. Everyone there is amazing. When Branden had his surgery (he had bone taken from his hip and grafted into his mouth), the principal called me and asked what we needed in terms of their help. He even offered to move the whole 4th grade from the 2nd floor to the 1st floor while Branden was healing. Unbelievable. Luckily, Branden healed so fast we did not have to do that.

There was one thing we did that made a big change to Branden, and that was the game we made up called: "What I like about you." Every morning we would drive for about thirty minutes to his school. On the way there, we would do this game where I would say something positive about him and he would do the same thing with me, and being as competitive as Branden was, there were quite a few positive things said. By the time he got to the school, he had heard so many good things about himself that he had a positive shield around him. As a mom, I thought to myself, *What can I do to make a difference in my child's life?* I decided to start writing children's books which focused on the message of acceptance. I then started going to schools and reading from my books and talking to children about the importance of not bullying someone because they were different. The age group I write for is 3-9, and it is amazing. They really do understand the concept of being careful with the words they use.

One of the things I did with my son as he was growing older and "attitude" and words started to hurt him was to go to the Internet and get statistics on how many children there are in the world born with a cleft palate/lip. When my son realized that every three minutes a child is born with a cleft palate and realized that he was not the only one, it "normalized" things for him.

I have been a big supporter of Operation Smile for many years. The work they do with children all over the world is just amazing, and to be able to change a child's life forever with just a small surgery is so wonderful. Branden's plastic surgeon, Dr. Garner, had also worked with Operation Smile. He had gone on many trips to foreign countries and worked on helping children with cleft palates. Branden always thought this was pretty cool, and it was a big plus; not all plastic surgeons do that and here we were in the hands of someone who really knew how to repair cleft palates and other deformities, and had stories to tell about his experiences. He also introduced us to a local family who had a boy with cleft palate, and I was able to talk to the mother and she gave me some good advice on how to get through the surgery, what to expect next, things to be aware of with his follow-up surgeries, etc.

- Living in California, we had most of our doctor follow-ups with the hospital at Stanford. When you go in the doors at these places, you really realize how fortunate you are. We saw children with challenges from "Cranial deformities" to Cancer. So many of us live in a bubble with no concept of what it means to be different. After one of our follow-up visits to Stanford right before Thanksgiving, I decided to share with my friends and family what I had seen at the hospital, and I wanted to share this with you too. It is not often that something makes such a deep impression on me, so here it is:

*Dear Friends & Family,*

*Today was Branden's Pre Op appointment at Stanford.*

*Branden's paperwork was completed, instructions given and any questions we might have answered. Branden is now all ready to go into surgery on Tuesday. My little guy is such a brave little trooper. He is very positive and a he has a "can do" attitude. He made sure the surgeon knew that he wanted the bone for the bone graft taken from his left hip, because as he said: "I don't want to weaken my right soccer leg."*

*As I'm sitting in the waiting room at Stanford Children's Hospital, I started to look around at all these beautiful little children all needing something done; they are all so very brave. As I was sitting there, I could not help but notice a young man and his little son who was in a stroller. The young man had his child turned towards the door where the nurses would go in and out. I noticed that when one nurse came out, she lovingly smiled and waved to the little boy as she gave the young father some paperwork. When he turned to leave, he covered his little child up with a blue blanket. It was very obvious he was hiding him. He carried a backpack with an oxygen tank on his back, and a long tube was going from the oxygen tank and under the blanket. The little boy was so used to being covered up that he did not even make any fuss. He simply put his little hand outside the blanket waving, as to say: "I'm here, I exist."*

*This wing of Stanford Hospital is a tough one to go to, because there are so many different deformities the surgeons deal with. I know that this is Thanksgiving, and I will give thanks for the wonderful surgeons and nurses we have. These people work tirelessly to change children's lives. Sometimes we get so caught up in the day-to-day that we forget to appreciate how really blessed we are to have a healthy child. Branden's surgery is really nothing compared to what you see at this hospital. It's like a hidden world. I hope God will perform a miracle for the young man and his son, and that all these brave little ones will have a wonderful Thanksgiving.*

*Hugs and kisses to everyone…Happy Thanksgiving*

*Love, Anita*

Being different is, of course, not always physical. We can be different in so many ways, but the important thing to teach our children and sometimes also our selves is that being different is perfect. I'm blessed to live in a place like Santa Cruz where people drive around with bumper stickers on their cars that state: "Keep Santa Cruz Weird." I'm in a community that really is very open to diversity, and people from all walks of life do seem to get along.

We teach our children to wash their hands, we teach them that two times two is four, we teach them to say thank you and please, but do we remember to teach them that the day they were born they broke the mold, and that they are special? You are unique and wonderful, different from everyone. We are born one of a kind, but we work our whole life to fit in with what's the norm. We are so fascinated with snowflakes, because no two are alike, and as children we want to be the first one to ever to find those two snowflakes that look exactly the same. But it is not going to happen, is it? The same way every snowflake is different, we need to allow ourselves to be different and cherish our own uniqueness.

I was discussing the fact that so many of us are guided by fear of "different" with someone the other day, and he commented that, "In a fish tank, the same kind of fish always stay together. They do not mix with the other fish. They are happy this way." Well, that's a fish tank, but is that what we want to create in our lives? Our own fish tank, a place we are comfortable in an ocean of sameness? We have our economic status, our standing in our community, our church, what car we drive, who our children are friends with, etc. Often, when we see a person who's different than us, we choose to go overboard with sympathy, or we politely ignore them. We feel uncomfortable, and do not want to make eye contact, or we do the exact opposite: we stare as if we are watching dogs fly. Whatever we do, our little ones are watching and learning. Teach them to celebrate different! Teach them to feel comfortable with different, not fearful of it. I truly believe that the day we embrace different as perfect is the day we can celebrate the end of bullying.

I was watching a rerun of *The Twilight Zone* one night and there was an episode that took place in an operating room. The doctors were working on the patient, and we could only see the back of the doctors and the nurses. After a while, they were going to take the bandages of this person's face to see if the surgery had been successful. But when the bandages came off, the nurses were sad for the person, and the doctor was upset. The patient was given a mirror and she screamed when she saw herself. She was hysterical and crying. She looked up at the camera and she was beautiful. Then the camera zoomed in on the nurses and doctor. When they took their surgical masks off, the lower half of their faces looked like those of pigs. Rod Serling (the creator of *The Twilight Zone*) wanted the viewer to understand that normal, and beauty, are a matter of perception.

My challenge to all parents and teachers is to teach our children about the importance of celebrating diversity. It is well known that in communities where families "normalize" the fact that we are all different, with our own uniqueness, children grow up feeling more safe, and accepting different is easy for them. I remember as a young girl I had pen pals all over the world. This changed my attitude from feeling afraid and suspicious of other cultures to thinking they were really cool. When I saw something on the news from India, I knew my friend Abu was there, or Linda in New Zealand, or Karen in South Africa. I wanted to understand and be knowledgeable about my friends' homelands. One thing I would encourage any teacher who might read this book to consider is to invite someone from another country to your classroom to talk about their culture. It could be before Christmas/winter break, and they could talk about how they celebrate the holidays, etc.

Encourage your child to develop friendships with children whose background is different from their own. Take your child to a restaurant that serves food from other countries. Go to cultural festivals, learn some new things from that country, and check out coins from another country. Do some fun games while learning about someone else's culture, like how many countries' national days do know, or why are they celebrating their national day. Learn to say "thank you" in ten different languages, etc.

Encourage generosity and sharing, and start early. I remember as a little girl, my girlfriends and I would sell candy at a stand and the money we collected we would donate to children in underdeveloped countries. It made us feel great to help out and curious about the people and the lands we sent the money too. Suggest to your school that they invite in a former Peace Corps worker or missionary to the school to tell about their trip and how it was to live overseas. Teach your children about different types of disabilities, and why certain things happen. Maybe one of their friends is in a wheelchair, and they may be wondering, "Why would someone sit in a wheelchair?" or "What is a cleft palate? How does that work?" The more we educate our children, the easier it is for them to deal with "different." Encourage your child to have an optimistic attitude, and teach them the golden rule: Treat others the way you want to be treated. It's a mind-opener for children, teaching them that even though different, we are all perfect.

Our children are growing up in a world so very different from the one we grew up in. The world is shrinking. My son plays his minecraft games with his friend in Florida and his friend in Australia at the same time, talking to them via Skype. More and more cultures are interacting. I was just at a seminar in Florida, and people from over thirty countries were there. This was not the norm only a few years ago. Sitting next to me was a man from Australia, next to him a guy from Germany, next to him a guy from South Africa, on my left side a girl from Sweden, next to her a girl from Holland, next to her a girl from Great Britain, and so on. We are more and more aware that the world is shrinking, so it leads us to one thing, and that is: It's all about choice. If we change our hearts and our thoughts, we can change the world. We have a choice to embrace different and make it an educational experience rather than something negative. I believe children are getting more and more aware of all kinds of different. I believe that being open, talking to and educating our children about everything from a disability one of their classmates might have to different cultures fosters an acceptance of different.

> *The world as we have created it is a process of our thinking.*
> *It cannot be changed without changing our thinking.*
> Albert Einstein

## Chapter 7
## Help your child find their ultimate bully shield

We talked in earlier chapters about how difficult it is to see our child being bullied; it is hard on everyone involved. However, the great thing we have today that we did not have only a few years ago is the Internet, and here we can find so many tools to help us. Like Olweus.org, stopbullying.gov.home, pacer.org/bullying, itgetsbetter.org etc., and I suggest you check out every single one of them.

However, what I feel is the ultimate bully shield is the opportunity we have at home to instill self-esteem in our children. As I said, we have already touched on this; however I feel so strongly about it that I feel we need to visit the subject on a deeper level. It is so important that our child understands how special they are. We must help them believe in themselves and at the same time teach them to understand the importance of others.

As our children grow up, they find themselves in so many confusing places along the way. They put themselves in little boxes. They might be very happy with their math skills and how they get along with other children, however, they can be really hard on themselves about, for example, their physical abilities. They might not be able to throw a ball at all. Around this time, they question a lot about themselves and they start to wonder: Am I good enough? What do my teacher and my classmates think of me? They start to compare themselves with others. They try on many "hats" to see how they can fit in, and they also pay a lot of attention to feedback they receive from others (including ugly comments from bullies).

However, media and teachers are also a big part of how they perceive themselves. They start seeing themselves in a certain place, and where they belong. That is why we must make sure that the place they arrive at in their own minds about their self worth is a place that is safe, comfortable, and a place where they know they are one of a kind! A place where they feel competence, where they know that they have the knowledge or skills to fill the qualifications for a particular situation, whether social, academic or physical. If they learn the opposite of this, it is hard work to help them see themselves otherwise; that's why it is so important to teach our children that our love for them is unconditional, that we love them no matter what. This makes them feel safe and ready for another day and it actually helps them to show love to others.

It is also important to be realistic about our children and realize that maybe they are hyperactive, are acting in a manner that maybe is annoying to his/her classmates. Instead of arguing about it and putting blinders on, accept it and help your child in developing more socially acceptable ways of behaving. If we as parents choose to ignore it, there is a very small chance the child will learn. We are the child's parent, but we also wear the hat of their closest coach. So when we have one-on-one time with them, we need to talk to them about both positive and negative behavioral traits that are important for them to develop. Let them tell you about examples they might have and together talk about the right choices in each example and why it is the right choice.

When you start having your one-on-one talks with your child, ask questions such as, "Why did you choose to do it that way?" or "How did it make you feel?" or "Can you explain to me in your own words why you made that choice?" or "Was it a good choice, or a not-so-good choice?" When they say things like, "I hate science, I'm just not smart enough," teach them to say "I'm capable, I'm able, and I'm doing my best." It is important that our children are aware of their strengths and weaknesses, and that we all have some things that comes easier to us than other things.

One of the things that were a challenge to get through my son's head was respecting personal space. He loved to hang onto people, and he could not understand that this was annoying. He liked it when kids would hang onto him; he thought it was fun play. Why they might not have the same enthusiasm about it was not something he understood. We had many conversations and discussions about that subject; I would say: "You need to understand that everyone needs their personal space. You need to stay at least one to two feet away from someone when you talk to them. If you would like to put your arm around a friend or classmate, ask permission. Not everyone wants you to hug them."

This was probably the one area my son really had a hard time understanding. He was amazing when it came to saying please and thank you. He was also really great at encouraging others; he loved to show someone how to do something and then encourage them to succeed. It was around this time we also started to learn about body language, what someone's expression meant, etc. However, some kids need more instruction and time to acquire the social skill of reading someone's expression, tone of voice or body language.

My son and I would do things like trying to figure out how someone was feeling, or what mood they were in. This was something we would do if we were sitting a stop light, for example. We talked about things that he could do for himself, and I would teach him things my parents had taught me, such as my dad always saying that you show who you are in your handshake. He would tell me not to give a limp fish handshake, and to make sure it was firm, but not too firm. We had a lot of fun trying out different handshakes. When he gave a "good" handshake and had good eye contact with the person he was talking to, he would at times come over and ask me if I saw that he had given a good handshake and remembered to look them in the eyes. He needed the encouragement and knowing he had done well.

Another thing we made a game of was posture. Of course, before you ask your child to learn about good posture, you will have to explain to them why it is so important, especially today with the amount of time children spend in front of the TV and video games. They need to understand how important it is for our backs and joints to stay healthy. It is also important for them to know how good posture makes people look better, more confident, and healthier. I told my son that when I was a little girl I would walk with a book on my head to make sure I had good posture. Being my son, he of course wanted to try that out. So we turned it into a game; if I saw him slouching, I would tell him. If he saw me do it, he would tell me.

One day we were grocery shopping and I was sorting through some vegetables and my son was on the other side of the store. Suddenly, I heard, "Posture." It sounded like a drill sergeant was after me. We both got a good laugh from that experience; I think I probably jumped a foot. There are fun games you can do too, like having your child stand with really bad posture, look down at the floor and say a lot of positive things, such as, "I feel so happy today, I'm in a really great mood." This will look so funny, as will having them stand up straight and say negative things. If this game is played around friends, everyone can participate.

As our little ones grow up, it is important to encourage them to explore and learn new skills; this again makes them feel more comfortable with themselves and allows them to have the feeling of being capable. At times, our children (like us) will experience stress. A really cute exercise for that is again to turn it into a game. Have them sit in a chair, pretending to be a bottle of orange juice (turned upside down). Have them close their eyes and feel all the stressful thoughts and anxieties as being on the bottom of the bottle (which, because the bottle is upside down, will be their little head). Then tell them you just opened the bottle and all the juice is flowing out, the "juice" being their stress. Have them shake their little shoulders as the stress is flowing out, and when they feel that it has come all the way down to their feet, have them stand up, do a little "shake dance," and make sure everything is gone. It is now time to refill the bottle with happy thoughts.

When your child feels safe and secure, they feel better about themselves and develop more and more self-awareness and self-esteem. It is important to let our children understand that we will often not get the exact outcome we want; that's life. Instead of, for example, blaming it on the referee in a game, tell the truth: "Well, maybe you just did not have your eye on the ball at that exact moment." That does not make you any less. When Thomas Edison was asked about the 700 times he was not successful in creating the functional light bulb, he said: "I have not failed 700 times; I have not failed once. I have simply succeeded in proving that those 700 ways will not work." Again, teach your child to look at a challenge as an opportunity and a learning experience. This gives them a way to evaluate the way they did it and come up with a different way of how they can make it work better next time. It's all in the attitude; Thomas Edison showed that to us, so remember that only a slight shift in our attitude can make an amazing change.

As we talked about in an earlier chapter, empathy is an important part of raising your child. It is important that your child understands others' needs, and how his/her behavior makes others feel. You are the one teaching them how to be aware and how to care about others; when others feel bad, you try to help them. Volunteering and being aware of others are great gifts to give your child. I believe it's never too early to start, and you will be so amazed with how soon they pick up on the idea of being helpful and showing kindness. Teaching them that it is better to give than to receive can be a difficult task, however, they need to understand that philanthropy is not just for wealthy grownups. You can teach your child that it will also make them feel good inside when they help others in need.

A way to start getting them involved is to help them find a charity that is important to them. At times, grocery stores ask you to donate a dollar for a charity. They then hang a tag up on the cash register. This is a fun way to allow your child to see his/her name and know that they are making a difference. Every Christmas since my son was about four years old, I would take him to a toy store and I would tell him that we were going to purchase four toys, three for some children his age that maybe would not get other gifts this year, and one for him. The first year, he just threw three toys in the basket and then spent a very long time finding something for himself. It was hard for him to purchase for someone he could not see or did not even know.

The years after went much better until one year he really realized the importance of taking time and choosing wisely, finally understanding the significance of what he was doing. If you do this, make sure he/she helps with wrapping the gift, and maybe even writes a nice card to go with it. Last year on Christmas Eve, my son and I went to a nursing home and visited with a person we did not know. We brought a magazine and some chocolate; the lady really loved the fact that she had someone visiting her on Christmas Eve.

It is so easy to be busy and forget about the needs of people around us. Therefore, it is (for me) important that I introduce my son to the needs of others. Organizations such as Operation Smile and St. Jude's Children's Hospital are great organizations for children to learn about. Oftentimes, schools will do charity work or put together "shoe boxes" that are sent to children in need. These are just a few suggestions of organizations you could have your child learn about, and maybe somehow get involved. Let your child be the one sorting through old clothes and toys and decide to give them to someone in need. Oftentimes it is so much easier to just do it ourselves, but allowing them to be the one giving away their things is empowering. Maybe your child would really enjoy helping at animal shelters, which would teach them to treat animals with kindness. Or they might want to help out with environmental causes, keeping our planet healthy. There are so many things your child can get involved with on a local level.

As my son was growing up, I would always count to three when there was something I needed him NOT to do, and of course he would stop at exactly two and a little bit. But he would stop. If we do not set limits for our children, they do not feel important. Being indifferent or trying to be their best friend does not help them on their journey of growing up. We need to encourage our children's sense of responsibility and nurture self-esteem. This will in the long run strengthen our relationship with our children.

When we teach our children the balance between receiving and giving, teach them to share, to be polite, give them tools with which to set boundaries, understand what acceptable behavior is, and make sure they have chores and work to do around the house, we are helping them on their journey of growing up. The reason I spent so much time on self-esteem and self worth is that this is the ultimate bullying shield, as well as a gift of long life. Yes, long life. Study after study has shown that people with a positive attitude and high self worth live longer and have better health.

It is very important for the child to learn ways to do things independently, to understand and appreciate their own ability to do something, have a positive opinion about themselves and know they have done the best they can. When they have positive thoughts about themselves, it is just the icing on the cake when they also receive positive reinforcement from other sources. A child who is independent will feel more confident about themselves, especially in situations when you are not there. When they are allowed to and can do things on their own, it gives them freedom to help other children. When they are allowed to help others, they develop confidence, compassion, and healthy self-esteem. When a child is confident and has a healthy level of self-esteem, they will automatically want to learn new things and take on new challenges. The key word here is, of course, healthy self-esteem. We certainly do not want to raise the child to be so self absorbed that they think of no one else but themselves and their immediate needs. That's why teaching them that there is always time for kindness is so important.

We talked earlier about daily positive quotes. A good source for fun, silly and, happy quotes for children is inspirational Dr. Seuss quotes.

Quotes can be found at: http://brightdrops.com/dr-seuss-quotes http://www.brainyquote.com/quotes/authors/d/dr_seuss.html

> *"And will you succeed? Yes you will indeed!*
> *(98 and ¾ percent guaranteed."*
> Dr. Seuss

# Chapter 8
## A great bullying prevention program that works

I have been researching the subject of bullying and how to prevent it, what works, what does not work, etc. There are a lot of suggestions and fabulous websites out there providing help to parents, teens, children, educators and others learn about the problem of bullying and what can be done about it. However, the program that I found that stood out amongst them all was the Olweus program. I contacted the organization and asked permission to share with you the outline of the program. Personally, I have no connection to the organization; I'm just excited about the opportunities that are out there for helping our children and our schools. I think this proven program could be a great resource for helping achieve our goal of safe schools.

There is a cost to the program, and often this is the reason schools do not get involved. However, if after you read up on this you feel this could make a change at your child's school, then bring it up to your school's principal. Or bring to their attention any programs you learn about that you think could make a difference to your child's school. It is not as much of which program as it is about why they do not have one.

The Olweus program is an evidence-based program (a Blueprint Model Program, as well as a Level 2 program for the US Department of Education), and federal funding is available to support schools in purchasing and implementing the program. There are all kinds of ways a school can get funding, from City Blocks grants, local businesses, local PTA organizations, school district funds, county health department funding, the US Department of Justice, the Office of Juvenile Justice and Delinquency Prevention, the US Department of Education, the Office of Safe and Drug Free Schools, and more.

The cost is a one-time cost, though sometimes a school finds it necessary to make a small order for material that has been lost. I really encourage you to read up on the program. There's a lot of information on their website. There are even free web seminars, where you can learn about different kinds of bullying issues, the effects of bullying etc. Thousands of schools throughout the United States have been trained to use the program. School personnel are happy to talk with others who are considering the program, and the information about who to contact is available on their web page. Anyway, I wanted to share with you some of the most-asked questions regarding this program:

**What is the Olweus Bullying Prevention Program?**

The Olweus Bullying Prevention Program (OBPP) is the most researched and best known bullying prevention program available today. Backed by more than thirty-five years of research and successful implementation in many different countries, the Olweus Bullying Prevention Program is a whole-school program that has been proven to prevent or reduce bullying throughout a school setting. The program is used at the school, classroom and individual levels and includes methods to reach out to parents and the community for involvement and support. School administrators, teachers and other staff are primarily responsible for introducing and implementing the program with the purpose of improving peer relations and making the schools a safer and more positive place for students to learn and develop.

**What are the goals for the program?**

To reduce existing bullying problems among students, prevent development of new bullying problems and achieve better peer relationships at school.

## What are the components of the program?

The program is not a classroom curriculum; it's a whole school system-change program at four different levels: School wide, classroom, individual and community. This program has been more thoroughly evaluated than any other bullying prevention/reduction program so far. The program is designed for students in elementary, middle and junior high schools. All students participate in most aspects of the program, while students indentified as bullying others or as targets of bullying receive additional individualized interventions. The exciting thing is that a large-scale evaluation involving more than 40,000 students produced the following documented results: 50% reduction in students' reports of being bullied and bullying others. Peer and teacher ratings of bullying problems have yielded roughly similar results. The program has shown reductions in students' reports of general antisocial behavior, such as vandalism, fighting, theft, and truancy. Improvements in classroom social climate, as reflected in students' reports of improved order and discipline, more positive social relationships, and more positive attitudes toward schoolwork and school. For students in grades 4-7, most of these positive results can be seen after only eight months of intervention work, given reasonably good implementation of the program.

The program is divided into 4 levels:

**School–Level:** Establish a bullying prevention coordinating committee. Conduct committee and staff training, Administer the Olweus bullying questionnaire school wide. Hold staff discussion group meetings. Introduce the school rules against bullying. Review and refine the school's supervisory system. Hold a school kick-off event to launch the program. Involve parents.

**Classroom-Level Components:** Post and enforce school-wide rules against bullying. Hold regular class meetings. Hold meetings with students' parents.

**Individual-Level Components:** Supervise students' activities. Ensure that all staff intervene on the spot when bullying occurs. Hold meetings with the students involved in bullying. Hold meeting with parents of involved students. Develop individual intervention plans for involved students.

**Community-Level Components:** Involve community members on the Bullying Prevention Coordinating Committee. Develop partnerships with community members to support your school's program. Help to spread anti-bullying messages and principles of best practice in the community.

During my research I was not able to find any other prevention programs with such an overall approval rate. Even if you just want to educate yourself, this is a great web place to get educated: www.olweus.org

**Who is Dan Olweus?**

Dan Olweus, who was born in Sweden, received his doctoral degree at the University of Umeå, Sweden in 1969. From 1970 to 1995, he was professor of psychology at the University of Bergen, Bergen, Norway. Since 1996 he has been a research professor of psychology affiliated with the Research Center for Health Promotion (HEMIL) at the same university. For nine years (1962-70), he was director of the Erica Foundation, Stockholm, Sweden, and a training institute for clinical child psychologists.

For approximately 40 years, Dan Olweus has been involved in research and intervention work on bullying among school children and youth. In 1970, he started a large-scale project which is now generally regarded as the first scientific study of bullying problems in the world. In the 1980's, he conducted the first systematic intervention study against bullying in the world which documented a number of very positive effects of his "Bullying Prevention Program" (e.g., Olweus, 1991, 1992, 1994; Olweus & Limber, 1999). Towards the end of the century, Dan

Olweus and his research and intervention group at the University of Bergen conducted several new large-scale intervention projects, again gaining good results. One of these studies forms part of an international project on bullying problems comprising researchers from Japan, England, the Netherlands, the USA, and Norway.

Olweus has received a number of awards and recognitions for his research and intervention work. In 2005, he was awarded the Queen Sofia of Spain Medal for his contributions as well as the "Honorary Prize" of the Faculty of Psychology at the University of Bergen. In 2011, he received the Distinguished Contributions to the International Advancement of Psychology Award, given by the American Psychological Association (APA), and in 2012, he received APA's award for Distinguished Contributions to Research in Public Policy.

Olweus' intervention program against bullying has gained both international and national recognition. Among other recognitions, the Olweus Bullying Prevention Program was selected as a Promising Program by the Center for the Study and Prevention of Violence, University of Colorado at Boulder in their Blueprints for Healthy Youth Development initiative. Furthermore, the Olweus Bullying Prevention Program was the only program against various forms of "problem behavior in school" that could be recommended for continued use by a

Norwegian expert committee evaluating 55 different programs in use in Norwegian schools (in year 2000).

When you go to their web page, you can find answers and suggestions that address many issues you might face in regards to bullying. This Organization is definitely one of the biggest gems I found during my research.

*The worst loneliness is to not be comfortable with yourself.*
Mark Twain

## Chapter 9
## An unexpected turn of events

WOW, what an eye-opener. As word got out that I was working on my anti-bullying book, I had many wonderful and interesting experiences. One of the things that happened was that people would start talking to me and telling me their stories. Some of the stories were so special that I decided to dedicate a whole chapter to them, and here they are:

I was invited to lunch with an acquaintance of mine. I had never been around her much, but she wanted to tell me a story. She said that she hoped I would consider including a story about someone who had *been* a bully and truly regretted her behavior. She said, "I have to tell you that when the subject of bullying comes up, I cringe. I know in my heart I was a bully. I had no reason to treat this particular girl the way I did. She was just an easy target; she had a handicap and she did not fit in. My friends and I made it a weekly goal to be nasty and cruel to her. Now when the subject of bullying is talked about, it almost makes me physically ill thinking about the way I was. I know the girl we bullied has probably moved on, and has a beautiful life, at least I hope she does, but I will always remember the way I treated her. I regret it and I have no excuse other than I was foolish, selfish and had a lot of my own issues. Whether she remembers me or not, I will and can never forget for the rest of my life what I did. I'm sorry for my behavior and I hope any bully that reads this takes note.

You might think it is cool, and that you make people laugh at someone else's expense, but trust me, twenty-five years later what I did still haunts me. Yes, a former bully can feel remorse and guilt, so if you are going down the path of thinking you are cool and powerful, know that those feelings will be short lived. Please take my advice and stop. You do not want this hanging over your head for the rest of your life. You might say that it is garbage and that people should not be so sensitive, but who are you to decide that? I was not what you would expect a bully to look like. I was popular, I came from a good home, I was pretty, and had overachieving parents, both well educated. However, though things were missing in my life, and I had a lot of my own turmoil, it was not okay for me to do what I did."

As she told me her story, her eyes watered and her voice cracked at times. I don't know if she had ever voiced this to anyone else. There was a part of me that was not sure what to do with the information. There were all kinds of feelings going through my head, from, "Of all the people in the world, I would never have guessed that she had been a bully," to "It's amazing how much good she is doing for the children today." The saying sure is true: "You can't judge a book by its cover."

As for me, I was having a hard time figuring out where I could possibly fit this in my book. It really did not go with what I had in mind to write about, so I figured I would fit it in front under the title: "An apology from a retired bully," or something like that. But she was not the only one with a story. More and more people started to come out of the woodwork, in the form of calls, Facebook, e-mails, etc. And when I visited one of the schools I read to, I discovered that a lot of the little ones had things to say too.

From one of the schools I visited, little Gracie (4th grade) had this to say:

"I will stand up for bullies. I know I am supposed to be writing a paragraph how bullying is wrong, but I know the real reason bullies bully. It's either because their parents are mean and they want to make other people sad, or scared, and not know what to do. The other reason is because they are so angry and want to take it out on someone else. The final reason can never be solved. They are rich so they are sometimes very snobby and they look down on others. In conclusion, bullies aren't always bad."

Megan (4th grade) said:

"Bullying is wrong. Bullies shouldn't act this way. They can really hurt your feelings and can hurt people. Bullies sometimes kick or punch other kids. My friends were playing together when a boy came and started chasing us. The boy then broke my friend's watch. She reported him to our teacher. He has never done anything to us again. I wish all bullies would stop acting this way. Bullies shouldn't be at schools, parks, and swimming pools. We could make Earth a better place with no bullies."

"Greg" was bullied as a child and decided to take matters into his own hands as the teachers back then were not educated about bullying and didn't have had the tools they do now. Here's his story:

"I was the oldest child in my family. Both my parents worked and had way too many things to deal with. The guy who bullied me was best friends with my cousin. It was embarrassing and hurtful. As I was growing up, I often got hit and beaten and one time they hung me up on a fence and I was not able to get down without ripping my clothes. When I got home, my mom noticed my ripped clothes and asked me what had happened. I told her I did not want her to say anything because it would only get worse. I live up north, so we have snow there, and one winter I was walking home and there was the bully standing in front of me. He threw me down on the ground and set on me for what seemed like hours, and when he let go I could hardly breathe. My face was red and I felt as if I was going to faint. When I got home my mom saw something was really wrong, and this time, she did not care what I said. She went and talked to the principal, and things got a little better after that. I was allowed to leave school a little earlier than the other kids, so at least the way home was safe. This was a turning point for me.

I made a decision that I would never be hurt like this again, and it did help that I grew a lot one summer. So then what I did was to hit first and ask questions later, and suddenly I was called a bully. Today the bully and I are good friends. He has never said he's sorry for what he did to me in middle school, but I have heard enough stories about his dad to know his life was not as easy as maybe I thought. His dad was known for being the tough guy that no one could take down, and he certainly did not want his boy to be a sissy. Anyway, that was then, and my advice to anyone who's bullied is to use the resources you have, older siblings, parents, teachers, coaches, etc. There are so many ways to get help nowadays. I do not recommend my solution to the problem. I did what I felt I had to do, however, I'm teaching my kids to walk away and to tell should something similar happen to them. Thank God it has not happened to them. The teachers are way more on top of things now."

Aurora (4th grade) had this to say:

"Bullying is not cool. I'm bullied a lot. Bullying is ugly. Okay, so draw a picture of a heart on a paper, crumple it, smash it, maybe even tear it. If that was somebody's heart, they were getting bullied. After that, flatten it out, sit on it, tape it, that's the bully saying sorry, but the damage doesn't go away."

Gabe (4th grade)

"Have you been getting picked on by a bully lately? Maybe you should try being nice to the bully. Sometimes if you play with a bully they might stop being mean. If it works there will be less bullies in the world. Try it now. Only you can stop bullying."

A poem by Jayden (4th grade) about bullying:

"Bulldoze bullying to make it instinct. If you don't believe me just Think, Think, And Think! When bullies are here, there is lots of fear, when not there, there's peace everywhere."

"Kris" was bullied all through middle school and wants to share her story and to say that everything will work out, so hang in there:

"I was bullied, teased, harassed, and humiliated as a child. I was tall, skinny and wore glasses. I was called 'four eyes,' 'owl,' 'and tooth pick,' and the name-calling was horrible. I was never hit physically, but I have to be honest, sometimes I wish I would have been hit, because then I would have had evidence to show. Being told you are just too sensitive does not solve the problem. My parents were loving and kind and wanted to support me, however, their solution was to change schools, which I did not want to do, as I did have one friend who I did not want to leave behind. She was also being bullied. She was a little round and was very bad in sports, and no one wanted her on their team. I would always tell people things were okay, and I told my parents that I wanted to stay at my school, and that everything would be better very soon. It never happened, and I cried myself to sleep many times. Now when I look back at the way things were, in one way I'm glad I did not change schools, but in another way I wonder if it would have been better. It is true, time does heal, and things will get better, however, my heart goes out to the children who are still getting picked on every day. Children should not feel that even adults cannot help them. Know that there are many places you can get help. Start with your mom and dad, teachers, the Internet, etc. As for me, I'm doing great. I have a beautiful partner who loves me, I have my own art business and my life is great. Hang in there."

Phoebe (4th grade)

"I hate to be bullied, I'm sure everyone does. When anyone gets bullied they almost always remember it for their whole life. When you get bullied you should feel bad for the bully. Normally when someone is a bully they are sad or trying to get a need met. When you get bullied here are some ways to stop the bully. You can walk away from the bully and tell an adult. If you want to talk to the bully, say something that is not mean and then the bully can't say something back. Or you can just hold your head high and walk away."

Rebecca (4th grade)

"I don't like bullies. In fact, no one does except bullies themselves. Reason you should not bully is: 1. It can hurt someone. 2. It's wrong. 3. You're being a bad student, classmate and friend. 4. You're being a bad influence for younger people. Don't bully."

Ilaria (4th grade)

"Do not bully it is not nice, tell whoever is bullying to stop, then walk away. Ignore him or her and go tell a yard duty, teacher or a parent. Try to make them happy, and you guys can be friends.

If they insult you, just agree with them. For example if they say your shirt is ugly, say YES IT IS."

Last year I participated in a business fair here locally. I was promoting my books and Boo Boo Bears (Boo Boo Bears are little bears filled with rice that you heat up in the microwave or chill in the freezer and use for any boo-boo. Check them out at wwwboo-boobear.org). A little girl came over to me to ask me the price of the book and was wondering if she could hold a Boo

Boo Bear. As I was talking to her, she told me she had had to change schools two times because of bullying. She was the most beautiful little girl ever! After a while, her mom came over and we continued to talk, and right before the event was over the little girl came over and purchased a book and a Boo Boo Bear. I wrote a nice note in the book telling her she was one of a kind and she was very special. Many months later, I was reading my book at a school, and a little girl was smiling at me the whole time. She said, "I have that book, and I have a Boo Boo Bear." I said, "That's wonderful," but I still did not put two and two together.

When I was done reading, the little girl came over to me and gave me the biggest hug. I told her she was one of a kind and wonderful, and she looked up at me and with that big smile, I realized she was the same little girl I had met months earlier! It made me so happy. She is now a student at a wonderful school. She is happy and all is well with her. This made me realize that even though, as a grown up, whether you are a mom, dad, aunt, uncle, cousin, or grandparent, if you just say a few positive words to a little child it can make a big difference in their life. Even a little praise here and there can really make a child shine. Sometimes we hear parents say that they don't want to praise their child too much, because they don't want it to go to their heads. Like everything else in life, there has to be balance, however, it is important to know that praise and positive reinforcement can help with so many behavioral things. When you praise your child for playing independently, praise them for being such a good listener, for waiting so patiently, or for cleaning up their toys, they notice that you notice that they are being good, which encourages them to try even harder, and when you start on pointing out the positive in these little ones' behavior, you will find it changes your day to one with more "sunshine."

*Things turn out best for the people who make the best of*
*the way things turn out.*
John Wooden

# Chapter 10
## Happily ever after

What an amazing time it has been writing this book. I hope you can find some guidance in it, and I hope you will make a difference in the world. You are awesome, you want change, and we can do it. The month of October is Anti-Bullying Month, and I spent the month visiting schools and reading my children's books about acceptance to many children, and I have to tell you I am so encouraged; there is so much good out there! So many wonderful, loving teachers, and so many great kids who are getting the message that we are all a little different, but all perfect. Their participation in the discussion about why bullying is not the right thing to do is unbelievable. I have found that most of the children I read to have an amazing outlook on what should be done about bullying. Their love and acceptance for each other is admirable. They are winners. If we can get the message out there that it's cool to be different and awesome to be kind, if we start teaching children at an early age, we will have a generation of children growing up being loving, kind and accepting different.

Writing this book was hard. The subject was intimidating, but so is everything before you really study it. Listening to the news about children committing suicide was depressing. However, I made a decision, and that was that nothing was going to stop me from doing something to make a change for the better. Our children are the most precious gift we have, and no one should be bullied. So I started my quest, and even if I only make a difference to one child, I have done something. I learned through my research, by visiting schools and doing interviews that every one of us can make a difference. I am more encouraged now than I have ever been. Meeting children at different schools has recharged my battery. These children are so ready to do what it takes to make a difference in the world. They want a better world for themselves and their friends, they are hearing our message and they will be the change we need. During October, I read to over 500 children, and again, I feel so encouraged.

Away from the subject of bullying, I wanted to end this book with some of my thoughts on happiness and things that have made my life such an adventure, and that is taking the time to get to know yourself, do your best and give yourself a break. In talking with hundreds of parents, grandparents, aunts, uncles and children and asking them what they wanted to share with me and what makes them happy, these are some of the things I have learned.

Our children are so unique, and as parents we want them to grow up and lack nothing. We want them to follow their dreams, be happy, find success and be loved. The one gift we can give them is optimism, and showing them unconditional love and raising them in an optimistic home makes children happy and gives them a "can do" attitude. When children feel connected to their family, friends, teachers, etc., they feel they belong. When they feel wanted, acknowledged and when they feel that they are not a nuisance to us, that's when they feel happy and joyful. There are so many examples of this, and I believe it is something parents really need to hear.

Like most people, my son and I have a pretty crazy schedule. However, there is one thing that is for sure: we always have dinner together. When we sit at the table, the one thing my son loves is when I tell stories from when I was a little girl about the crazy stuff we did. I grew up with a loving mom and dad and two siblings (a lot older than me), so my stories are mostly about my friends and I. My son will listen to the same story over and over again because it makes him laugh, and he loves to laugh. He knows my friends and so enjoys hearing about our fun times. I don't believe my son is unique in this regard; I believe if you start telling stories from long ago (remember, ten or twenty years to a child is forever), your children will enjoy them. So share your "ancient" stories from when you were a child; your children will love it, and it will build memories.

I read once that a study over a timeframe of fifty years showed that social connections might be the most important contributor to happiness, which tells us that the Internet and video games as the only form of entertainment is not a good thing. Let your children not grow up in a cocoon where they hardly know the names of their cousins. One thing my son and I do is take a car trip every year. It gives us hours in the car together. Of course he wants to play his DS or watch a movie, but we also have a rule about "our time." You might say, "Well, I have three children and you have one," but still, the one-on-one time is crucial for the child. My son and I use the car; you might sit on the porch.

During your one-on-one time, spend time having fun, but also explain to your child what "makes you tick" and what is important to you. It is so very important that your child understands what really matters to you, what you value, and by telling them and showing them by your actions what is important to you, it teaches them about you and also give them a chance to internalize those values.

As I was growing up, my parents always made sure I understood I was a unique individual, my own person. Independence was very important trait my parents gifted me. I was allowed to make my own choices and at the same time had to deal with the consequences of my choices. Age- appropriate independence is very important for children; if we do not give them that, they could push away in order to try to find their own selves, who they are.

Independence is very important, but so are structure and guidelines. It is important that we set fair and clear expectations, and we must stick to them. If you do not follow through with the consequences you tell your child, you're opening yourself up to many challenges later on. One of the things children do not like about grownups is that they feel grownups do not keep their promises. One little girl told me about her mom "promising" she would stop smoking. To this little girl, a promise is a promise, so when she saw her mom smoking at a party a few weeks later, she was devastated. Instead of saying, "I promise," the mom could have said, "I will do my best," or even "I will consider it." This would not have made her break her promise, which was heart wrenching to the little girl. Kids keep tabs on us, and they measure how often we break a promise. Unless you intend to keep your promises 100% of the time, choose another word to use than "promise."

One of the things I really cherish being around so many little ones are the things they teach me, their outlook on life, their simple, yet at times so very deep, thoughts. The relationship with our children is a two-way street; they learn from us and we learn from them. They open our eyes up to so many new things;

they help us see the world and other people through their eyes, in new ways. It's such a gift.

Being loving parents, we so often want to give our children everything they want. However, that instant gratification and getting everything they want is not realistic; it's an easy fix and I do not know any parent that at one time or the other has not fallen into that trap. The real world does not work that way. Our children might get upset if they do not get something right now, however, we cannot control our children's happiness, only our own. It is important for them to be able to experience frustration, sadness and anger. It is okay for them to have some alone time to sort out their feelings and develop coping skills for the real world. My son will sometimes say, "I need alone time now" and he goes and takes a break.

Our children read us as an open book. We might not think so, but they do. The other day my son asked me what was the matter, and I told him I was fine. He said, "Really mom? Remember, I know you." So I told him I was a little concerned about going to the doctor. He told me that I should follow my own advice and know that fear is not a good thing, and that I should stay positive and know that whatever happens, we'd deal with. "And until then, we will not worry, " he said. This again tells me that when I'm happy, he's happy, and that he is listening.

My son was telling me the other day that he wanted to quit playing a certain sport. I told him that I really wanted him to find the sport that he could call his own, a sport that he really felt passionate about, however, I would not allow him to quit the team until the season was over. He thought I was not very nice right then, so I told him Rome was not built in one day. It takes time to master anything; you have to practice and practice some more. I told him we do not give up on the team, we stick with it. He was not happy and he told me so. However, I felt that teaching him that giving up when things are difficult would not prepare for the future challenges in life. He was welcome to try out for another sport after the season ended, but not before. After a few days of on and off again negotiating and realizing that I would not change my mind, he owned it and made it work.

As I told you before, the one exercise my son and I have worked on for years is to daily voice our gratitude. We also never do negative self talk, like "I can never do anything right." We focus on our gifts, positive thoughts and things we can be grateful for. Today we have daily positive quotes sent to our cell phone. We read them out to each other and sometimes talk about what we think they mean for us.

What we did was to make a conscious decision on a deep level to really realize what a gift life is. You might say to yourself: "I will be happy when this or that happens." If you do, you miss out on the NOW, this moment. I remember one time around the age of twenty or so, an old man overheard me telling my friend that I could not wait until the weekend (this was on a Wednesday). He quietly said, "Young lady, don't wish your life away." This stuck with me. It made me realize that each day is a wondrous gift. Of course, at times in my life, like everyone else, I have not felt that. However, even if the only thing you have to be grateful for is that you're breathing, then that is a beginning. Little by little, start adding to it, and pretty soon your list will get longer and longer. If we start looking at life as a game, an adventure to be experienced, and not as a problem that we need to solve, we will feel more relaxed and content, and when we really and truly realize that no one really cares about us as much as we might think, it is liberating.

You can not worry about what others think about you. They are probably worrying about what you think of them. There are two of my girlfriends that I admire a lot when it comes to this. They truly do not pay any attention to snide comments or negativity, criticism or anything similar. They just accept and realize that is that person's opinion, so they move on. Life is too short. Harboring dislike or revenge does nothing good for us. It is important that we acknowledge our feelings when someone hurts us. To sweep them under the rug certainly does not do us any good. We need to honor how hurt we are, because repressing our feelings just means they will reappear when another situation triggers a similar response. But negative emotions can sap our energy, so we must never give someone so much power over us that they can have an effect on who we are.

You will feel much happier if you choose to ignore an unkindness and respect yourself enough to know that you deserve to feel good and be happy. Again, how you feel reflects on your child's happiness. Just simple day-to-day things can make a huge difference. You do not have to go and sit on a mountaintop somewhere. You can enjoy your favorite music, go for a walk, do some exercises, read a book, or learn new things. There are so many things that can help you live happily ever after, and one of the things besides exercise that can make you feel great is getting enough sleep. Oftentimes, we do not sleep enough and this can affect us in a negative way. Enough sleep is important for our children and also for us.

Remember that onboard an airplane, when you travel with a child, the stewardess tells you that if the cabin pressure drops and the oxygen masks drop, you need to put yours on before you put your child's on. The reason for this is that at 37,000 feet you have eighteen seconds to get your mask on before you pass out. I had no idea I had only eighteen seconds, until one day on a business trip the lady next to me told me that. It made me take notice and realize, like the oxygen mask, as parents we must make sure we take care of ourselves and not run ourselves into the ground. Taking care of ourselves is not selfish; it's actually a deep sign of caring for others, because the more you take care of yourself, the more you can serve others.

I hope you have enjoyed my book and have learned some things that would be helpful for you in dealing with bullying, as well as some suggestions on how to maybe make things a little easier for yourself. I hope you realize your power, and that you don't let anyone tell you that you cannot have the life you want.

My wish for you is for courage, love, happiness, friends, family, perfect health and as much money as you need to make your life the way you want it to be. I wish for you that you realize that FEAR stands for "false evidence appearing real," and that each day you enjoy the knowledge that everything might not work out exactly the way you planned it, but you have a choice to make the best out of everything and to live in the moment and make your life's journey a blast. Like my "American" grandma said when she was telling me that she had cancer, and it was fatal: "I have lived my life to the fullest, I have celebrated every holiday and birthday, I have travelled and done all that I wanted. I have helped my fellow man, I appreciate having been a mom, and I have enjoyed the blessing of having grandchildren. I watched the sunsets as well as the sun rises. Do I wish I had

had more money and travelled and done even more? Maybe, but I'm satisfied with where I have been and been grateful for every little bit I have received. Live your life with gratitude and you will be blessed beyond your wildest dreams."

# The Paradoxical Commandments

People are illogical, unreasonable, and self-centered.
Love them anyway.

If you do good, people will accuse you of selfish ulterior
motives.
Do good anyway.

If you are successful, you will win false friends and true
enemies.
Succeed anyway.

The good you do today will be forgotten tomorrow.
Do good anyway.

Honesty and frankness make you vulnerable.
Be honest and frank anyway.

The biggest men and women with the biggest ideas can be
shot down by the smallest men and women with the smallest
minds.
Think big anyway.

People favor underdogs but follow only top dogs.
Fight for a few underdogs anyway.

What you spend years building may be destroyed overnight.
Build anyway.

People really need help but may attack you
if you do help them.
Help people anyway.

Give the world the best you have and
you'll get kicked in the teeth.
Give the world the best you have anyway.

Kent M Keith

# Sample letter to your State Senator

Your Name
Your address,
Phone # and e-mail address

DATE:

Go to:
http://www.senate.gov/general/contact_information/senators_cfm.cfm and find your State Senator by entering your city and zip code.

The Honorable (full name)
United States Senate
Washington DC, 20510

Dear Senator (Last name):

Cyber bullying seems to be becoming a bigger and bigger problem, and as a parent this is very concerning to me.

Our state of_____ still does not have a law against cyber bullying.

I'm asking your help in bringing light to this issue. Protecting our children from cyber bullying and other forms of bullying should be a priority for anyone. Even though our state has a bullying law, it does not include anything about cyber bullying. Thank you for your consideration of my viewpoint. I feel strongly this is a very important issue, as this is a matter of protecting our children from harm.

Sincerely,

## Sample letter to your child's school principal

Your Name

Your address,

Phone # and e-mail address

DATE:

Principal's Name

School

Address

Dear Principal...........................

My name is.........................I'm the parent of .....................who is in ..............grade.

My son/daughter has been bullied at school and I'm requesting an investigation from your office into the matter and that a solution be found that stops this from happening again.

The incidents took place on the following dates: .................. and on date:...........................

(Give brief description of what took place, who bullied/assaulted your child, include who witnessed the incident.)

The first incident was reported to .........................................

And the 2nd incident was reported to.........................................

Unfortunately, nothing has changed. It is the school's responsibility to provide my child with a safe environment in which he/she can learn and grow as a student.

I would like to meet with you in person to discuss this matter. I'm available next week on:...............

In the meantime, should you have any questions, feel free to call me at: (insert phone #)

Sincerely,

# Sample letter to the US department of Education

Your Name
Your Address
Phone number and e-mail address

TO:
U.S .Department of Education
Office of Civil Rights
Attn: Customer Service
400 Maryland Ave SW
Washington DC 20202

Date:

Dear Secretary of Education, Arne Duncan. (Double check who the secretary is at the time you send out the letter.)

I would like to file a complaint with the US Department of Education regarding School district #____

I feel they have failed in protecting my child from bullying at:_____

Elementary/ Middle/ High school in the state of ____City of_____

My son/daughter has been bullied for _____years/months now, and as of now he/she is in ____grade.

During the last ____months, she has been bullied and harassed because of his/her_____

I contacted the school, discussed the issue with the teacher/principal on 3 different occasions:

Date:_____( I reported the incident to:_____)
Date:_____(I reported the incident to:_____)
Date:_____(I reported the incident to:_____)

My daughter/son has been bullied at school during school hours. Even though I have notified the school staff on many occasions regarding this matter, they have failed to address the bullying and harassment and are continuing to allow it to go on, and are doing nothing to prevent it from recurring.

Should you have any questions, feel free to contact me at my address above.

## Sample note of apology for bullying

Dear.................

I am very sorry for bullying you, I know what I did (be specific) was wrong. I should not have done what I did. I truly regret my behavior and I understand my behavior was very hurtful to you. If someone had treated me that way, I would have felt sad, and I'm sorry I made you feel that way.

I promise you I will make other choices next time I feel upset or angry, and not take it out on others.

Again, I'm sorry for my poor choices.

Sincerely,

*Anita Telle*

StopBullying.gov
https://www2.ed.gov/.../bullying
www.cdc.gov/viole
www.regionalmentalhealth.org/r_violence&bullying.php
www.olweus.org
www.fbi.gov/.../cyber-bullying-psa

www.ingramcontent.com/pod-product-compliance
Lightning Source LLC
Chambersburg PA
CBHW062013200326
41519CB00017B/4788